ABOUT T.

Greg Rosen is a political columnist for the *Scotsman*, Vice-Chair of the Fabian Society and Chair of the Labour History Group. He has worked as a civil servant and for the UK's largest trade union.

His previous books include: *Old Labour to New* (Politicos Publishing, 2005) and the *Dictionary of Labour Biography* (Politicos Publishing, 2001).

For the LHG team past and present:

JC; MS; PL; SP; TG; AH; AR; AT; EC; JS

SERVING THE PEOPLE

CO-OPERATIVE PARTY HISTORY

from Fred Perry to Gordon Brown.

ISBN: 978-0-954916-14-5

Printed and bound in Great Britain by
Biddles Ltd, King's Lynn, Norfolk

FOREWORD

When I first joined the Co-operative Party, I was aware of its proud history. I shared its conviction that social justice can best be achieved through co-operative action.

Throughout our history as a nation, the co-operative movement has not only provided services on which ordinary people rely, but has strengthened the very community bonds from which we flourish. Today, the Co-operative Party's commitments in an interdependent world make its work more relevant than ever.

The Co-operative Party stands for social responsibility, for global decency and for people having a say in the running of their communities.

These are the values that I share. I wish the Co-operative Party well in its 90th year and I look forward to working closely with it in the future.

Rt. Hon Gordon Brown MP
Prime Minister

CONTENTS

INTRODUCTION

When Sam Perry, father of tennis star Fred, founded the first Co-operative Party headquarters ninety years ago in a London still suffering Zeppelin raids, few would have predicted that within thirty years it would be the third largest party in Parliament, with more MPs than the Liberal Party, or that on its ninetieth anniversary, a Co-operative Party member would become Prime Minister.

It was his father's appointment as the first Co-operative Party National Secretary that brought nine-year-old Fred Perry from Lancashire to London – and more precisely to the Brentham estate, a pioneering Edwardian co-operative housing scheme in Ealing which subsequently became an architectural model for the more famous Hampstead Garden Suburb. For Sam it was a good commute to where he was setting up a party head-office near Charing Cross Station. For Fred, Brentham was 'paradise after the bleak streets of the north because everyone in the garden village had use of the Brentham Institute and its cricket field, football pitch, tennis courts, bowling green and – an important thing to me – table tennis facilities. It was there that I first became interested in watching and playing sport, because it was all on the doorstep.'[1]

Had his father's role in the Co-operative Party not brought Fred those opportunities, Britain might well have been denied the world-championship victories that he brought in table-tennis (1920) as well as his Wimbledon treble (1934-36). Indeed, had his father not had the opportunities afforded him through his involvement in the co-operative movement, first in Stockport and then in Birkenhead, Fred Perry might well have grown up a cotton-spinner. For that was what his father Sam had become at the age of ten, when the death of his own cotton-spinner father had required him to give up his scholarship to the five-hundred-year-old Stockport grammar school to help feed the family. It was his involvement with the Stockport Co-operative Society, of which he was elected president, which gave his talents as an organiser the opportunity to shine through.

By the turn of the century, the co-operative movement had built up trade of almost £50 million[2] (which at today's prices works out at approximately £3.9 billion[3]). Its investment was managed and profits distributed in the interests of nearly two million working-class members, all of whom had their own democratic

1   Fred Perry, *An Autobiography*, (Hutchinson, 1984), p 15

2   G.D.H. Cole, *A Century of Co-operation*, (Co-operative Union, 1944), p 375

3   Jim O'Donoghue et. al, 'Consumer Price Inflation Since 1750,' National Statistics, http://www.statistics.gov.uk/articles/economictrends/ET604CPI1.pdf

voice within the enterprise. For Perry, the co-operative movement was a way of life, as much a part of him as Methodism, temperance and playing the cornet. The co-operative movement's activities extended into almost every facet of life. Jim Craigen[4] recalls 'as a boy of eight…going with my parents to whist drives organised by the co-op – it was a social thing.' The co-operative insurance and funeral services meant that it even provided for the afterlife. Even James Bond was a co-op man: Sean Connery's first job was as a delivery boy aboard a co-op milk van from the Edinburgh depot at Fountainbridge. Writing in 1926, Labour's future deputy leader Herbert Morrison, an active member of south-east London's Royal Arsenal Co-operative Society (RACS), gives a flavour of the immense breadth of co-operative provision: 'so seriously do my wife and myself take our co-operative principles that not only are the bulk of our household needs purchased as far as possible from the co-op, but the house itself has been decorated and a new fireplace constructed by the RACS. We bank with the co-op and I am insured by the co-op.'[5] It was to defend these activities from hostile legislation that the co-operative movement began to engage with the political process.

It was Sam Perry's world which Harold Campbell, Perry's successor-but-one as party secretary, evoked in a 1947 pamphlet:

'Force of circumstances was the father and the co-operative movement the mother of the Co-operative Party. The movement began as an experiment in self-help, by the simple expedient of a few people buying in bulk at wholesale prices, retailing to themselves at current market prices and disposing of the surplus, by retaining some of it collectively, as capital for development purposes, and distributing the bulk of the rest among themselves in proportion to the amount each had purchased from the common pool (the stock). Here was a genuinely co-operative effort in thrift, born of necessity; a device to stretch one's miserable weekly pittance as far as it would go. It was practical, it was canny, it was essentially realistic. An ideal, an ethic, a philosophy grew out of the main stem of realistic self-help.[6]

Though Herbert Morrison's RACS fireplace installation department has long since closed, the values of self-help, personal responsibility, democracy and solidarity that drew the Perrys and millions of others into the co-operative movement, and from which the Co-operative Party was forged, still fire the soul of the party. They remain for Gordon Brown to draw on today.

---

4   Craigen was a Co-operative Party MP 1974-87. Interview with the author.

5   Herbert Morrison in *London News* May 1926 cited Bernard Donoughue and George Jones, *Herbert Morrison* (Weidenfeld and Nicholson, 1973), p 65

6   Harold Campbell, *Wanting and Working* (1947), p 3

FIRST SERVICE

Like the original Labour Representation Committee of 1900, from which the modern Labour Party evolved, the Co-operative Party was conceived not so much as a putative party of government but as a pragmatically rooted parliamentary pressure group.

The co-operative movement which founded and funded the party had been growing steadily since the success of the Rochdale Pioneers, who founded their shop on Toad Lane in 1844.[7] With the subsequent creation of the North of England Co-operative Society, launched by 300 individual co-ops across Yorkshire and Lancashire in 1863, co-ops were on the march. The burgeoning numbers of co-operatives had in fact been sending delegates to a Co-operative Congress as long ago as 1831. Indeed, at the 1832 Congress Robert Owen himself moved a resolution urging that, 'co-operators as such are not identified with any religious, irreligious, or political tenets…' It reflected Owen's scepticism of parliament, which, even with the Great Reform Act passed that very year, was hardly representative. It was to be nearly half a century before most working-class men got the vote and the first General Election in which all men and women over twenty-one could vote was not until 1929.

Nevertheless, despite the scepticism of Owen and others, the co-operative movement campaigned strongly on issues that its members believed affected them. Thus they fought against the requirement to pay income tax on the money set aside from profit for distribution as dividend and in support of free trade against Joseph Chamberlain's tariff proposals, which would have increased the cost of food.

By 1880, the Co-operative Congress had created a Parliamentary Committee to lobby Parliament on behalf of co-operative societies on relevant issues. Although a handful of Liberal MPs were members of the co-operative board, it was not long before the committee was recommending that its impact would be greater were it to have MPs speaking up directly for it in Parliament.

The scepticism this proposal encountered was rooted partially in frugality: at that point MPs were unpaid and there was concern at whether funding MPs

---

7   The first British co-operative societies are thought to have been formed during the 1760s by the Weavers' Society at Fenwick, Ayrshire and at corn mills in Woolwich and Chatham. Others followed with varying degrees of success, including those established by Robert Owen at New Lanark and by Thomas Hirst at Huddersfield.

would be the most effective use of members' money.[8] In 1900 the co-operative movement declined overtures to join the trade unions, the Independent Labour Party (ILP), the Marxist Social Democratic Federation (SDF) and the Fabians in founding the Labour Representation Committee. That same year a proposal for direct representation in parliament was defeated at the Co-operative Congress by 905 votes to 409. Nevertheless, the 1901 congress chose to debate issues outside the immediate realm of co-operative interests, namely old-age pensions and the state of the railways. Despite vocal opposition from some prominent Liberals, the 1907 Co-operative Congress was to vote in favour of direct political representation in parliament. It also voted against simply joining the infant Labour Party. The mood was summed up by the president of the 1908 Co-operative Congress, TW Allen: 'If parliament means anything for the public welfare, for the problems of preventable misery, for the hungry and unemployed, for the banishment of social darkness, then our place is within its walls.'

The practical challenge remained persuading sufficient of what were by then more than sixteen hundred individual societies to pay for a political party, which as these were individual self-governing entities, required considerable leg-work. It was the First World War that changed opinion amongst co-operative societies. The conduct of the war exposed a profound ignorance among ministers, politicians and most administrators as to the scale and significance of the co-operative trade within Britain. While the officials of political parties and trade unions had been made exempt from conscription, those of the co-op had not. In one case it meant that a society had all but three of its hundred and two employees conscripted. In addition, the government imposed an 'excess profits tax' on co-operative surplus and designed a rationing supply system based upon a shop's previous trade, preventing co-op retail societies from expanding (the Co-operative Party was to ensure the system was different in the Second World War).

The 1917 Co-operative Congress repudiated those such as Liberal activist EO Greening who claimed that the best model for securing political support for co-operative interests was the multi-party approach then being used by Channel tunnel campaigners. Given that the Channel tunnel took nearly eighty more years to be completed, the Co-operative Congress of 1917 seems to have been exceptionally sensible. Instead the Co-operative Congress voted again to create a Co-operative Party. And this time, galvanised by the refusal of Lloyd-George to meet members of Co-op Parliamentary Committee (it is said he opted to meet

---

8   Despite a number of attempts during the 19th Century to secure salaries for MPs, it
          was not until 1911 that this was agreed, due largely to pressure from the Labour Party.
          Salaries were not introduced for ministers until 1937.

the Jockey Club instead), co-operative leaders secured sufficient support amongst individual societies to secure the attendance of delegates from more than five hundred societies at the founding conference at Westminster Central Hall on 17-18 October 1917.

The other political parties had agreed an electoral truce while the wartime Coalition lasted, and even before any party staff could be appointed, the Co-operative Party found itself with the chance to fight a by-election at Manchester Prestwich, where thirteen separate co-operative societies had shops. The candidate was Woolwich-born Henry May, fifty-one years old and secretary of the old Co-operative Congress Parliamentary Committee since 1908. He polled a respectable three thousand votes as against the eight thousand votes for the Coalition candidate, and held his deposit.

During the summer and autumn a two-room head-office was secured in a small club, called the Emerson Club, at 19 Buckingham Street in London, just off the Strand. Staff were swiftly appointed: party secretary Sam Perry, an organiser, and Sue Greenway, who was, as she said at her retirement thirty-two years later, 'the office staff'. Hailed by many as the man who made the Co-operative Party, Perry 'nearly always succeeded in applying the art of persuasion where forceful demands would have brought certain failure and resistance,' a colleague recalled.[9] He even managed to persuade young Fred to forgo the pleasures of demon drink until the age of twenty-one (though he was assisted by the promise of £100 and by Fred's own memory of being hung upside-down from a clothesline by a drunken alcoholic uncle).[10]

When the Coalition Prime Minister David Lloyd-George called the 'Coupon Election' in December 1918 (which saw opposition Liberal and Labour candidates pulverised at the polls by candidates possessing a 'coupon' of endorsement from Lloyd-George) ten Co-operative candidates were fielded and one, Alfred Waterson (a thirty-eight year-old Derby-born railwayman, rail union district secretary and town councillor) was elected at Kettering. Several others also polled well. During 1920, the Co-operative Party fought two by-elections. At the first, in Paisley, the Co-operative Party almost defeated former Liberal leader HH Asquith, who having lost his seat in 1918, was attempting to return to the Commons. The Co-operative Party national secretary – Sam Perry – was also runner-up at the second by-election, this time in Stockport.

At the 1922 election which saw Lloyd-George turfed out of Downing Street, four of the eleven Co-operative Party candidates were elected including Alf Barnes (East Ham South), AV Alexander (Sheffield Hillsborough), Tom

---

9   Extract from forthcoming biography of Fred Perry by Jon Henderson.

10   Fred Perry, *An Autobiography*, p 24

Henderson (Glasgow Tradeston) and Bob Morrison (Tottenham North). Waterson lost Kettering and never returned to parliament. The new MPs however would all play important roles in the future of the Co-operative Party.

AV Alexander would become the Co-operative Party's first minister, first cabinet minister, and eventually its first and so far its only Earl. The son of a Somerset blacksmith, when in 1886 his father died he was barely a year old. He and his sisters were brought up in Bristol by their mother, a corset-maker. Leaving school at thirteen to work as a local government clerk, he became Secretary of the Somerset County Council Local Government Officers Association. Apart from service in the Artists' Rifles during the First World War, where he rose to the rank of Captain, he worked in Somerset, where under the influence of his wife he became a Baptist lay preacher and joined the local Co-operative Society. It was while working as chief clerk of Somerset's education department that in 1920 he successfully applied for the post of Secretary to the Parliamentary Committee of the Co-operative Union. In turn, this provided the springboard for his adoption as candidate for Sheffield Hillsborough and his election as an MP.

Alf Barnes was the son of a Silvertown docker. With the help of the LCC School of Arts and Crafts, he became a notable silver and goldsmith. He was also an ILP, co-operative and trade union activist and his political talents had played a central role in persuading the Enfield Highway and West London Co-operative Societies to merge with the Stratford Co-operative Society (of which he was president 1915-20) to create the London Co-operative Society. Barnes became its president in 1920, serving until his election to parliament three years later.

The third new MP, Tom Henderson, had been a Glasgow City Councillor for the previous four years. He had worked for thirty years as a ship-joiner on Clydeside and in Belfast having been apprenticed to a cabinet-maker on leaving school at eleven. Henderson's win at Glasgow Tradeston in 1922 was the first parliamentary victory for the Co-operative Party in Scotland.

The last of the four, Bob Morrison, had roots in the co-operative movement going back to the cradle: his father an Aberdeen railwayman, had been a lifelong co-operator. A teacher and Middlesex County Councillor, he was, like Barnes, active in the London Co-operative Society and served on its management board.

In 1922 the Co-operative Party went beyond its original defensive posture and adopted for the first time a formal programme to supplement its general position as an advocate of co-operative interests. At its heart was support for free trade and the abolition of indirect taxation. It also advocated graduated direct taxes, the assumption of responsibility for full employment (or maintenance) by the government, the public control of monopolies and the nationalisation of land. To avoid conflict with a potential Labour alliance, it judiciously avoided pronouncing on the ownership of industry. On broader questions it foreshadowed the progressive measures of future Labour governments, calling for non-contributory old-age pensions below the age of seventy, equal educational opportunities for all, generous maternity and infant welfare provision and scientific agricultural development. Internationally it reflected shared Labour and radical Liberal priorities calling for a fully representative League of Nations and parliamentary control over foreign affairs. It also favoured the democratisation of all public and civil services and proportional representation.

The 1923 election was dominated by the Conservative plan to introduce import tariffs, which would have increased food prices. It was an issue which went to the heart of the Co-operative Party's raison d'etre. When the ballots were counted, Conservative Prime Minister Stanley Baldwin had lost his parliamentary majority. In the hung Parliament which followed Ramsay MacDonald became the first Labour Prime Minister, prudently bolstering his minority government with ministerial appointments from outside the Labour Party fold. MacDonald's Cabinet included a former Brigadier-General, ex-Conservatives such as Lords Chelmsford and Parmoor and Liberal grandee RB Haldane. The Co-operative group of MPs had expanded to six (ten candidates having stood). Sam Perry had won back Kettering and another candidate had been elected at Glasgow Partick. Of these six, four found themselves brought into MacDonald's governmental tent, albeit at lower ranks (AV Alexander as junior minister at the Board of Trade and Barnes, Morrison and Perry in unpaid PPS positions).

The 1924 election, which saw a swing to Baldwin's Conservatives after the fall of MacDonald's government, saw the new MP and two of the six existing Co-operative MPs defeated (including Sam Perry). MacDonald (now Leader of the Opposition) seized the opportunity to bind the five-strong Co-operative Parliamentary Group into the Parliamentary Labour Party. He appointed Barnes and Henderson Opposition whips and chose Morrison as his own PPS.

THE LABOUR ALLIANCE

GDH Cole in his centenary history of the co-operative movement argued that 'there was no possible room for a second entirely independent working class party on a really national scale side-by-side with the Labour party of 1918.'[11] The Labour Party was already operating nationwide when the Co-operative Party was founded and the resources available to the Co-operative Party to build its campaigning infrastructure fluctuated with the level of individual society affiliations – when income slumped they cut political affiliation to protect the 'divvy' to members.

It was not the intention of the Co-operative Party to contest every seat against Labour – though local rivalries meant that electoral battles did happen. Thus at the 1923 election in Paisley the Labour candidate came fourth but split the vote, so that the Co-operative Party candidate (who came second) missed defeating Liberal leader HH Asquith. The Co-operative Party's objective was to push government policy in a direction more favourable to the interests of the co-operative movement and its members. Its leaders always saw this as a task best achieved in partnership with the Labour Party, but believed that without a separate and distinctive tail the dog would not always wag in the right direction. Their fears had been confirmed by the failure of the Parliamentary Labour Party to protect co-op interests during the First World War.

At the 1919 Co-operative Party conference, National Secretary Sam Perry had called for a federation of Labour, trade unions and the Co-operative Party under the banner of a 'New Democratic or People's Party'. At the 1921 Co-operative Party conference he returned to the theme declaring: 'Only by active co-operation with our friends in the trade union and Labour movement can we achieve the objects we have set out to obtain… we come of common stock.' He was clear, however, that it should be a partnership in which the Co-operative Party's distinctive concerns would gain voice – rather than one in which they were merely subsumed.

Labour also represented the aspirations of many of the same people for whom the Co-operative Party spoke, though with an important difference. Labour's trade union base represented what was an overwhelmingly male unionised manual workforce. The Co-operative Party represented the interests not only of co-operative producers but also of consumers. In consequence, right

---

11   GDH Cole, *A Centenary of Co-operation*, (Co-operative Union, 1944), p 317

from its inception, women had a far greater role within the Co-operative Party than any other and the Co-operative Women's Guild was one of the most influential organisations within it.[12]

Nevertheless, many of the wider policy issues raised at Co-operative Party conferences during the 1920s and 1930s were similar to those discussed in the Labour Party. There were the same demands for better public services, tackling poverty and an internationalist approach to foster peace. This informed the Co-operative Party view of public ownership. As Alf Barnes, then the president of the London Co-operative Society as well as an MP, explained in a 1925 speech: 'We are in politics, first, to defend the interests of the consumers, and, secondly, to use our political power to substitute collective ownership in industry in the place of private ownership... The Co-operative Movement does not accept the principle of buying out private enterprise; it competes it out of existence.'[13] For Barnes, moreover, collective ownership was not state ownership but co-operative ownership, which on the basis of the chronic inefficiencies then afflicting so much of Britain's privately owned industry, was assumed to be inevitable. Barnes also sought to advance the case for a more formal alliance with Labour: 'The Co-operative Party must play its part inside the Labour Party, and this means the extension of the principle of mutual aid in trade to mutual aid in politics, the dividend in the latter case being healthy housing conditions, complete education, economic security, good government, international peace...'

It was against that background, with Co-operative Party MPs having already served in a Labour-led government and holding positions within MacDonald's Labour team, that a partnership agreement was reached with the Labour Party. Ratified at the 1927 Co-operative Party conference in Cheltenham and known as a result as the 'Cheltenham Agreement', it provided for local Co-operative Parties to affiliate to Constituency Labour Parties with voting rights relating to affiliation fees. As Jim Craigen[14] later observed in a lecture he gave on Co-operative Party history, 'the Co-operative Party was thereafter bound to play second fiddle although it would also be able to use its own bow'.

The Labour alliance was not universally welcomed. The involvement of active Liberals and Conservatives at a senior level in a number of co-operative societies (for example in Leeds and Huddersfield) meant that the affinity of the

---

12   Admittedly, despite the high proportion of women activists, not until three women were elected in 1945, did the Co-operative Parliamentary Group cease to be all-male.

13   Alfred Barnes MP, *Co-operative Aims in Politics: an address delivered in Manchester to the Pioneer Group on 29th January 1925*, (Co-operative Union, 1925).

14   Craigen was a Co-operative MP 1974-87.

movement at a local level with the party was never universal. Some societies were not affiliated in consequence. In Northern Ireland, such was the dominance of co-operative societies by Ulster Unionists that an informal truce was agreed: the Co-operative Party did not demand the affiliation of Ulster co-operatives and, in return, the Unionists agreed not to sabotage the affiliation of the wider movement to the party.

At the next General Election (1929) the Co-operative Party fielded twelve candidates. Fred Perry's father was one of them, standing at Kettering against the Conservative MP, Sir Mervyn Manningham-Buller. Sir Mervyn was the scion of a long established Northants Tory dynasty. His own son Sir Reginald was destined to be the Tory Attorney-General and Lord Chancellor whose attempt to ban *Lady Chatterley's Lover* in 1960 earned him a footnote in satirical history as Bernard Levin's 'Sir Reginald Bullying-Manner'. Sir Mervyn's granddaughter Eliza became head of MI5 in 2002. Fred Perry turned twenty the day after polling but – though too young to vote – proved an energetic campaigner who accompanied his father to public meetings and would often sit on the platform. His other job as he recalled in his memoir was, 'to go around the factories and kiss all the girls – not a bad assignment'. The public meetings though could be more arduous: 'We had a rough time of it because in that part of the country the hunting set flourished and Labour was a dirty word. Troublemakers would show up at meetings in dinner jackets, determined to have some fun from the back of the hall and shouting things like, "which flag do you stand for, Perry, the Red Flag or the Union Jack?" It was a spread out constituency, containing ninety-eight towns and villages, so we had to plan six or seven meetings a night. The dinner-jacketed hecklers and our other opponents would attempt to jostle and delay us at each one in the hope that by the time we got to the last – and biggest – meeting our supporters would have got fed up and gone home.' It got so bad that a supporter named Joe Starmer, a former middleweight boxing champion and Lonsdale belt holder who ran a car hire business in Kettering, had to provide minders: 'If anyone gave persistent trouble he would find himself dumped into a dustbin at the back of the hall.'[15]

The election result saw victory not only for Perry but also for a record eight other Co-operative candidates. When Ramsay MacDonald formed a minority government on 5 June 1929, AV Alexander became the first Co-operative Cabinet Minister. Alexander's rise had been remarkably swift. As one observer remarked, 'he climbed the ladder of fame at a rate which considerably exceeds the normal speed of ascent of that steep incline'.[16] Like Ernest Bevin, then the boss of the

---

15   Fred Perry, *An Autobiography*, p 25-26

16   TN Shane in *The British Labour Party Vol III* by Herbert Tracey (ed), (London, 1948). p 61

giant Transport and General Workers' Union, he was one of the few leading working class politicians of the era to come from the West Country.

Gaining a reputation for knowledge and courtesy, his talents had led him to be tipped by the *Daily Mail* in 1928 as the 'designated President of the Board of Trade', a role that would have given him a great deal of scope to promote the Co-operative Party's political ethic.[17] But it was to the post of First Lord of the Admiralty that MacDonald appointed him: he became the man in charge of the Royal Navy. Meanwhile Alf Barnes and Tom Henderson became senior government whips, Bob Morrison continued as PPS to MacDonald and Sam Perry became PPS to the President of the Board of Trade.

To have already secured a voice in the corridors of power was a significant achievement for a party barely a decade old and with but nine MPs. AV Alexander earnt admiration from unexpected quarters (Winston Churchill included) with his handling of complex naval issues at the Admiralty. One of Alexander's major achievements, in addition to keeping the lid on the ever-present risk of a naval arms race, was to reform the system of naval officer recruitment to make it easier for working class sailors to secure promotion from the ranks. But with Alexander's hands full looking after the Royal Navy and two others in the whips office, the three most senior Co-operative MPs found their talents and energies diverted into channels where they had difficulty addressing the consumer issues which had brought them into parliament in the first place.

MacDonald's second Labour government was a tragedy. It was the most successful Labour government yet, and the first government without Conservative involvement to have lasted more than a year since the Liberal governments before the First World War. But the inability of MacDonald's Cabinet to agree on a solution to tackle the rising tide of unemployment in the wake of the 1929 Wall Street Crash and the Great Depression that followed precipitated the resignation of the government. To the shock and dismay of his colleagues MacDonald then took it upon himself to form a 'National' government with Conservative and Liberal support, taking half a dozen of his senior colleagues with him.

Alexander, Perry and the other Co-operative members of the government joined the overwhelming majority of their Labour colleagues in Opposition. Supposedly the 'National' government was a temporary expedient that would last only until the untenable position of Sterling vis-à-vis the Gold Standard had been resolved. But when Sterling crashed off the Gold Standard, MacDonald fought an election as the leader of the 'National' government. It was an electoral triumph for MacDonald and his supporters in the Conservative and 'National

---

17   Cited John Tilley, *Churchill's Favourite Socialist*, (Co-operative Union, 1995) p 26

Liberal' and 'National Labour' Parties. Arthur Henderson, who took over as Labour Party Leader following the departure of MacDonald, had remarked earlier that year to Sidney Webb that he saw 'Alexander, Morrison, Dalton, in that order [as] the most promising political leaders.' However not only Henderson himself, but Alexander, Herbert Morrison, Hugh Dalton, and indeed every single member of the Labour Cabinet apart from the septuagenarian George Lansbury, were ejected from the Commons at the election of October 1931. The Opposition (Liberal, Labour and Co-operative) Parties were almost annihilated. All the Co-operative Party MPs save one, Willie Leonard at Glasgow St Rollox, lost their seats.

If the electoral catastrophe of 1931 had deflated the case for a Co-operative Party in the eyes of the retail and wholesale co-op movement, then the agenda of the Conservative-dominated National Government soon reminded them why it had been set up in the first place. Neville Chamberlain, spurred on by the Retail Pharmacists Union, had already banned the payment of a 'divvy' on national health prescriptions dispensed by co-op drug departments. The great right wing press barons, Lords Beaverbrook and Rothermere, instigated a co-ordinated onslaught in their respective newspapers against the co-operative movement, arguing that small shopkeepers were being crushed by what they contended were unfair tax advantages held by co-ops.

The National Government set up the Raeburn Committee to look into taxing co-operative trading surpluses – a direct threat to the level of the co-op dividend. Despite a vigorous campaign at public meetings, a National Co-operative Petition of 2,343,654 signatures and detailed evidence to the committee, new tax measures were driven through by the National Government as the 1933 Finance Act. With only one MP, there had been little that the Co-operative Party could do. While a Conservative-dominated government remained in office, it was clear that the co-operative movement would suffer continued threats to its operations from vested interests in the private sector. The central task for the Co-operative Party was to rebuild its strength and, in partnership with Labour, to rebuild the credibility of progressive government.

The 1935 General Election saw a welcome resurgence, with nine of twenty Co-operative candidates elected, including those who had served in MacDonald's Labour government such as AV Alexander and Alf Barnes. In the meantime, however, the pacifist Labour leader George Lansbury had thrown in the towel, unable as he was to countenance rearmament to combat the threat of fascism. With none of the other heavyweights in the Commons, it was the little-known former Postmaster-General Clement Attlee who had succeeded him as Labour's leader. Not that they knew it at the time, but it meant that neither AV Alexander, nor either of the Labour rivals whom Arthur Henderson had mentioned (Herbert Morrison and Hugh Dalton) would ever be Prime Minister.

Alexander was nonetheless one of the half dozen most senior figures on the Labour front-bench. With the gathering darkness of Nazi aggression clouding the political skies Alexander played a crucial role in galvanising the Co-operative Party and the wider Labour movement into facing up to the need to confront Hitler. In 1936 Alexander warned the Co-operative Party annual conference: 'I prophesy that unless you deal with [Hitler] now, in two year's time Germany will be in a position to say to you, "This is where you get off."' It was Alexander who, with Labour MP (and future Chancellor) Hugh Dalton, was instrumental in changing the Parliamentary Labour Party stance from a pro-disarmament and anti-militarist position to one backing British rearmament. In common cause with his fellow former First Lord of the Admiralty, Winston Churchill, AV Alexander accused the National Government of a 'crass blunder' in giving in to Hitler's demand to build U-boats, which Germany had been specifically banned from constructing under the Treaty of Versailles. In March 1938 Alexander and Churchill mounted a joint attack on the failure of the National Government (by now led by Neville Chamberlain) to build sufficient new destroyers to protect Britain's vital merchant shipping from U-Boats.[18] As a Co-operative MP, Alexander knew all about Britain's reliance on imported food and raw materials. When the Commons debated the Munich agreement it was Attlee who opened for the Labour Opposition and Alexander who wound up the debate.

The outbreak of the Second World War split the Co-operative Party as it split much of the British left. During the 1930s, all too many British Conservatives deluded themselves that the Nazi jackboot was aimed solely and squarely at the Communist posterior and that, in the words of the senior Conservative MP Sir Henry Page-Croft, General Franco was a 'gallant Christian gentleman'. This made some Co-operative Party members reluctant to support intervention in a war to save Poland (governed by an authoritarian right wing regime) from an invasion from a Germany that (following the signature of the Molotov-Ribbentrop Pact) had now formally allied itself with the Soviet Union. They included one of the Co-operative MPs defeated at the 1931 election, Fred Longden, who claimed that the war was 'a clash of rival imperialism' and in an article for *Co-operative News* (30 March 1940) accused 'British imperialism of crimes equal to those perpetrated by Hitler'.[19] But as a whole, the Co-operative Party conference echoed AV Alexander's more patriotic note.

When Neville Chamberlain was forced out of Downing Street in May 1940, it was AV Alexander whom Churchill chose to succeed himself as First Lord of the Admiralty in the new Coalition government. It was thus a Co-operative MP who

---

18   John Tilley, *Churchill's Favourite Socialist*, (Co-operative Union, 1995), p 45

19   Thomas Carbery, *Consumers in Politics*, (Manchester University Press, 1969), p 44

would lead the Royal Navy through the great Dunkirk evacuation, and who would unsuccessfully advise Churchill against two of the great Naval blunders of the war: the decision to send the battleship *Prince of Wales* and the battlecruiser *Repulse* to defend Singapore against the Japanese without vital air cover and the failure to insist that the RAF lend its long-range bombers to protect merchant shipping from U-boats in the mid-Atlantic. Though he did not always follow Alexander's advice, Churchill had sufficient confidence in his First Lord for Alexander to remain in post throughout the wartime coalition. He also enjoyed a great deal of popularity with ordinary sailors, with whom he spent a great deal of time on visits to naval bases and aboard ship, on occasion playing the piano at their 'free and easies'.

Though not the Co-operative Party 'leader', by the end of the war, AV Alexander had become one of the pre-eminent figures in British public life. In the public mind, he was the 'Mr Co-op' of politics, even though as First Lord of the Admiralty he had had little scope to put distinctive Co-operative Party ideals into practice. With the surrender of Nazi Germany on 8 May 1945, the Labour and Liberal Parties decided to withdraw from the coalition. Churchill formed a Conservative government, comprised predominantly of National Government-supporting MPs elected in 1935. The Co-operative MPs joined Clement Attlee's team in the General Election battle that summer and Alexander used a party political broadcast during the campaign to re-assert the distinctive values of the co-operative movement: 'The Co-op is the people's main defence against monopoly. For many commodities the Co-op is the only challenge to the giant trusts. Lord Beaverbrook, the Tory campaign leader, threatened last week that if a Tory government is elected there will be legislation directed against the co-op – against the standard of life of the small man and woman who is a co-op member.'[20]

The Co-operative Party election campaign, organised by former party organiser Jack Bailey, who had succeeded Sam Perry as National Secretary in 1942, secured a record twenty-three MPs. Bailey, a former South Wales miner who had won a scholarship to the London Labour College, was more philosophical than Perry and played an important role in encouraging a broader policy vision for the party.[21]

AV Alexander found himself re-appointed as First Lord of the Admiralty in Clement Attlee's new Labour government – but promotion was to come within a year. In 1946 when Attlee merged the posts of the three services ministers then

---

20   John Tilley, *Churchill's Favourite Socialist*, (Co-operative Union, 1995), p 63
21   Bailey had served as the first full-time secretary of Bradford Co-operative Party before
      moving to Enfield on his appointment as National Organiser of the Party.

in Cabinet (first Lord of the Admiralty, Secretary of State for Air and Minister of War) into one, it was Alexander who was appointed to fill this new role as the first Secretary of State for Defence. Alf Barnes was appointed Transport Minister – a senior position even if not a cabinet one – which he occupied throughout the Attlee government. Willie Leonard, that lone survivor of the Co-operative Party MPs at the 1931 election, became a junior minister at the Ministry of Supply, where he served for the next two years.

THE PEOPLE'S INDUSTRY

The battle over nationalisation

To the Co-operative MPs elected in 1945, as to the wider Labour movement, the failures of unreformed capitalism were clear: the depression, vast cyclical unemployment, needless poverty and squalor, inadequate investment by complacent management, and poor employee relations. During the 1930s, co-operation was trumpeted in pamphlets and on the Co-operative Party conference platform as the best way to 'solve the problems of unemployment and poverty' but the rhetoric and idealism was not followed up with detailed blueprints. At the same time Co-operative Party left-wingers (such as the pro-Soviet former MP Fred Longden) had argued that cooperation and capitalism were incompatible – that capitalism saw co-operation as a threat and would therefore introduce discriminatory laws – and that therefore the abolition of capitalism was required for co-operation to flourish. As one voice put it at the 1936 Co-operative Party conference: 'We must socialise the banks, otherwise unless we own the banks, the banks will own us.' The anti-co-operative measures of the 1930s National Government, prompted by the campaigns of Lords Beaverbrook and Rothermere on behalf of small shops, had lent credence to these neo-Marxist views and demands for public control or ownership of land, water, fuel, finance and transport were passed at Co-operative Party conferences but with no consideration as to the form such public ownership would take or of the risks inherent in a burgeoning bureaucratic state.

Central to the arguments of those who advocated public ownership was the assumption that planning offered a superior way of running an economy than the market. Though the appalling human rights record of the Soviet Union was recognised by most on the left, many believed that it was more efficient at producing tractors and ball-bearings than the inefficient capitalist West. This was an assumption Co-operative Party members shared not only with Labour figures like Hugh Gaitskell and Nye Bevan but also with the new generation of 'middle way' Conservatives around Harold Macmillan and 'Rab' Butler. The nationalisation programme of the late 1940s would become part of what would be called the 'Butskellite' consensus of the 1950s.

If, during the 1930s, the Co-operative Party's domestic policy programme was vague, then the Labour Party's programme was equally so. Once Attlee assumed office it became clear that the Labour Party's commitments to nationalisation lacked any workable blueprints, or bluntly any detailed implementation plans at all. Indeed the only minister who had given any serious thought to this issue was Herbert Morrison, who had, as Transport Minister in Ramsay Macdonald's 1929-31 government, created the London Passenger Transport Board to run nationalised tram, bus and tube services in Greater London.[22] The civil servants who drafted the legislation for nationalising the 'commanding heights of the economy' thus took the nearest model they could find to hand – Morrison's LPTB – which was itself heavily influenced by the model used for the BBC, created by the Conservatives in 1926.

This model, designed for running transport in London, was enlarged, with no thought about how it would relate to ordinary people. It was, in the famous phrase of Labour MP Douglas Jay, a Treasury minister 1947-51, the era when 'the man in Whitehall knows best'. Sidney Webb had warned Labour against going down this road back in 1923 in the speech to Labour Party conference where he had talked of 'the inevitable gradualness of our scheme of change'. He had also said that Labour should 'insist... that government should at all points be heavily democratised; that it should be, wherever practicable, entrusted to the local representatives of the community rather than to the necessarily centralised departments at Whitehall; that in every branch the widest possible sphere should be assigned to the voluntarily assisted consumers' co-operative movement...' It was an admonition few appeared to remember. Morrison indeed was one of the few senior Labour figures to exercise caution over the creation of these new bureaucratic behemoths, raising the issue of whether more localised municipal control might not in some circumstances be more appropriate. It was a battle he was destined to lose.

It was from the Co-operative Party that the first sustained and coherent concerns were raised about the Attlee government's conception of 'public ownership'. They were concerns rooted in the very fibre of the Co-operative Party and a salutary reminder that the distinctive political philosophy of the Co-operative Party brought with it from its roots in co-operative societies even at that high tide of labourism. Back in 1929 AV Alexander had penned a short explanation of the Co-operative Party approach for the *Encyclopaedia of the Labour Movement*:

> *'In harmony with the declarations of the Rochdale pioneers, the party stands for a widening and deepening of the education of the people, the scientific development of agriculture, and the communal ownership of the land. It is able to deal with questions in the light of the cumulative*

---

22   Municipal London government – the London County Council – at that time covered only inner London making it impractical for it to become the responsible authority.

business experience of the movement covering eighty years, and whilst, as indicated, working in close harmony with the Labour Party, applies the test of that practical experience of trade and industry to all legislative proposals... That a parliamentary majority for collectivism will come is certain. The question will then have to be decided as to whether the realisation of collectivist policy shall be through state socialism and national ownership, by a system of Guild Socialism or Syndicalism, or whether it shall be upon the volition of free local democracies. There is always the danger in the regulation of everything by the State of bureaucracy on the one hand, and of the shedding of responsibility by citizens at the ballot box on the other. The Co-operative Party therefore, while certainly favouring the national ownership of the great services of the nature of monopolies, works for an extension and development of a Co-operative collectivism which springs from an educated rank and file rather than by the imposition of the state.'[23]

RG Gosling, director of the Co-operative Wholesale Society, had written in his 1946 Co-operative Party pamphlet *The Political Consequences of Co-operative Progress* that 'the co-operative method has been called the "middle way." Between the viciousness of capitalism and the evils of dictatorship in economic affairs is the path of democratic co-operation'.

Growing concerns at the structure of the newly nationalised industries were raised in a Co-operative Party pamphlet published in 1947 entitled *Wanting and Working*. It was penned by Harold Campbell, the thirty-one year-old Co-operative Party assistant secretary.[24] He demanded 'a co-operative community, not an anthill' and 'the limitation of overall state ownership and administration to the key industries with as wide a field as possible open to voluntary association based on socialist principles.'[25] He argued:

'If socialism is to end at nationalisation, or at public ownership administered through the state, co-operators are more radical than socialists. The kind of society that co-operation entails is much less "totalitarian" than that. The glory of human society is in its diversity, not in any uniformity. If the object of democracy is to identify government with the people ever more closely, then there must surely be an extending

---

23   AV Alexander MP in *Encyclopaedia of the Labour Movement*, HB Lees-Smith, (ed), pp
        183-184 (Caxton Publishing, 1929)

24   In 1963 he succeeded Jack Bailey as Co-operative Party National Secretary.

25   Harold Campbell, *Wanting and Working*, (1947), pp 13-15

devolution of authority from the centre. If a further object of social democracy is to maximise economic and political freedom, consistent with social well-being, we should be prepared to experiment boldly with different forms of voluntary association.'[26]

Campbell's concerns struck a chord with many in the co-op movement, such as Co-operative Party MP Tom Williams who warned the 1949 Party conference of the 'danger of socialism becoming bureaucratic,' and the authors of *The Socialisation of Coal-mining*[27] who recommended the abolition of the National Coal Board and the area system and entrusting coal production to co-operative societies of mine-workers self-governing within definite limits. But they found little resonance amongst the wider Labour movement. The Co-operative Party was not strong enough to win a battle over this issue without the full support of the co-operative movement as a whole. In 1949 such circumstances arose.

In 1949, in preparation for the next election manifesto, the Labour Party published *Labour Believes in Britain*, a document containing proposals for the nationalisation of the industrial assurance industry. This would have entailed nationalising not just such household names as Pearl Assurance and Prudential but also the Co-operative Insurance Society, which had been a part of the co-operative movement since 1867. Advocates argued that Pearl and the 'Pru' were making money at the expense of working-class families, and that the plethora of competing insurance firms were wasteful and inefficient. Riled at the failure of senior Labour figures to value the integrity and efficiency of the Co-operative Insurance Society, the co-op movement united in defence of the organisation that amongst other things provided the insurance for all the co-op shops.

Tense negotiations followed and the Labour Party conceded a wholesale change in policy: instead of advocating the nationalisation of the insurers, both private sector and co-operative, it would instead advocate the mutualisation of the co-op's private-sector rivals. It was a Co-operative Party victory, but one which earned it the enmity of a swathe of hard-left Labour MPs who would not forgive it for interfering with their nationalising zeal. They included Ian Mikardo[28] who made a notable attack on the Co-operative Party in a speech at Aberdare and James Carmichael who wrote a stinging attack on the Co-operative Party in the journal *Forward!*

---

26   Harold Campbell, *Wanting and Working,* (1947), pp 12-13

27   A C Stewart and W P Watkins.

28   Ian Mikardo was a leading left-wing Labour MP and proponent of nationalisation. A frequent speaker at the *Tribune* rally at Labour conference, he served on Labour's National Executive Committee for most of the period from 1950 until 1978.

The Co-operative Party National Secretary Jack Bailey responded in the *Co-operative Party monthly newsletter* of April 1953: 'Does Mr Carmichael imagine that the transformation of an industry from private... to public ownership, substitutes magic for sound commercial practice?'[29]

For Bailey, the issue was clear – the Co-operative Party simply could not have allowed the proposal to nationalise the CIS to stand. 'We should not stand by idly... while co-operative democracy was served up at the banquet of state-worshippers,' he wrote.[30] The CIS is around to this day (now as part of the Co-operative Group) and as of July 2007 administered more than £20 billion of life, home and motor insurances, pensions, with-profits bonds, critical illness products and ISAs on behalf of 4.7 million customers.

In reality, it was not just the Co-operative Party that put the brakes on the Labour left's quest to nationalise a further 'shopping list' of industries; it was the electorate. So small was the Attlee government's majority after the 1950 election (at which the number of Co-op Party MPs was reduced to eighteen) that neither the Labour government's pledges to nationalise sugar and cement, nor the pledge to mutualise the life assurance industry, could be implemented.

What it had done, however, was to bring into the open Co-operative Party concerns at the nature of Labour's nationalisation programme. The 1951 Co-operative Party conference voted for the Party National Committee 'to consider the relationship of the co-op movement to nationalisation and public ownership generally,' and to draft a plan setting out 'the means of applying co-operative methods and principles in appropriate services and industries... [and] giving the consumer an adequate voice in the conduct of publicly owned enterprise'.

Before anything could happen, Clement Attlee called another general election, and the government's majority evaporated entirely. The Co-operative Parliamentary Group was reduced to sixteen MPs, now sharing the Opposition benches with Labour and Liberal colleagues, while Winston Churchill returned to Downing Street at the head of a Conservative government.

The first draft of the proposed policy statement, entitled *The People's Industry*, produced by Co-operative Party research officer Bert Oram, was eventually published in the spring of 1952. It asked 'is nationalisation, as we have known it hitherto, conferring too much power on central agencies of the state and giving too little power to the workers in the nationalised industries and to the consumers of the products and services?' It anticipated Tony Crosland's attempt in his book *The Future of Socialism* to persuade the Labour Party to remember the difference between ends and means. Oram's paper offered the view that 'there is a tendency... to think that socialism always means

29   Jack Bailey, *Co-operative Party monthly newsletter*, April 1953, p 20
30   Jack Bailey, *Co-operative Party monthly newsletter*, January 1953, p 10

nationalisation; that to advocate more and more nationalisation is to advocate more and more socialism. "Nationalisation" may only be a convenient new slogan to avoid the necessity for new thinking.' It was an era in which memories were fresh of the very real 'inadequacies of the private sector regimes which were replaced,' and in deference to Labour Party sensitivities Oram's paper emphasised that the Co-operative Party 'has supported and will continue to support nationalisation in those industries where it is the best form of social ownership'. The implication, however, was that there were areas where it was not and that a 'diversity' of provision would be better: 'A community which organised all its social and economic processes according to one centrally determined pattern would be a drab and inefficient affair. It would fail to evoke enthusiasm and initiative from its members.' Oram's examples consisted of those areas where there was already a co-operative alternative, which Oram believed the state should leave well alone. He argued that 'socialism does not seek to eliminate all forms of competition. It seeks only to ensure that it serves desirable ends and promotes the good of the whole, where hitherto it has been a weapon of economic aggression'. Oram's vision was of a society where 'control is democratic because it is placed in the hands of the representatives of many people rather than in the hands of a few people privileged by their wealth'.[31]

Ultimately, the different sovereign committees of the co-operative movement proved unable to agree on the detail of the proposals, thwarting the original intention to produce an agreed and comprehensive Party policy. Nevertheless, the Co-operative Party's rejection of centralised state nationalisation as a panacea for the challenges facing Britain provided an important intellectual outrider for those within the Labour Party who from the mid-1950s began to question the role of Clause IV[32] of Labour's constitution in the pantheon of Labour priorities. Its resonance can be seen more recently in the phrasing of Tony Blair's revised Clause IV of the Labour Party in 1994 – Oram, in fact, sent in a copy of his pamphlet to assist Blair's deliberations.[33]

While the co-operative movement was considering Oram's paper, the still mutual Co-operative Insurance Society (CIS) bought a quarter of a million shares in the United Steel Companies following the denationalisation[34] of steel by the Conservative government, inflaming the likes of Ian Mikardo even more. But as the Co-operative Party Chair Lord Peddie told delegates in a guest speech to the 1953 Labour conference, there was never any prospect of the Co-operative Party

---

31   *The People's Industry*, (Co-operative Party, 1951).

32   Its commitment to nationalisation.

33   Interview with Lady Oram.

34   As privatisation was still called in those days

conceding so important an issue: 'We in the co-operative movement... have no desire and indeed no intention, of allowing ourselves to be the central figure at our own funeral, no matter how friendly the undertaker might be.'

When in 1956 a glamorous young ex-MP named Anthony Crosland published his book entitled *The Future of Socialism*, it echoed the Co-operative Party critique of nationalisation:

'It is not enough to tell people that they are working for the public good, nor even that they should... This may be seen from the experience of nationalisation. The miners and the railwaymen are in fact working for the public good as well as for themselves... and there are no shareholders or private profits to 'expropriate' the fruits of their labour. Yet this appears to make only a limited psychological difference and neither industry has a contented atmosphere.[35]

---

35   Anthony Crosland, *Future of Socialism*, (Jonathan Cape, 1956), p 108

THE STORM IN AN EGG-CUP

Though the 1955 election had seen the Conservative majority grow, the Co-operative Party had managed to buck the trend and actually increased its MPs to nineteen. Indeed, the tenacity of the Co-operative Party in fighting its corner was increasingly acknowledged within the Labour Party, but not always for the right reasons. The success of Co-operative Party organisers in securing selection for their candidates in winnable seats, including at several crucial by-elections, caused resentment not only from Labour left-wingers, who feared the political consequences of a more powerful Co-operative Parliamentary Group, but also from trade union barons who resented the challenge to their own control of candidate selections.

When Clement Attlee announced his resignation as Labour leader on 7 December 1956 the media descended upon the by-election campaign in the safe Labour seat of Greenock, to see who the Labour candidate in that election would back as Attlee's successor. But there was not, in fact, a Labour candidate. Dickson Mabon, the telegenic thirty-one year-old doctor and Glasgow University Union *Observer Mace* debating champion, who found himself asked to pronounce on whether Attlee's successor should be Morrison, Bevan or Gaitskell was in fact the candidate of the Co-operative Party. Mabon announced his backing for Hugh Gaitskell. It was a happy conjunction: Mabon won the seat and Gaitskell won Labour's leadership. But jealousies were rife – Mabon and other new young Co-operative candidates were accused of not being 'real' co-operators but 'carpet-baggers'.

In 1955 British co-operatives had reached their peak in terms of market penetration. They were operating thirty thousand retail shops, and had a 20% food retail market share, a 12% non-food retail market-share and a membership of some thirteen million people. Facing growing competition from the 'multiples',[36] the 1955 Co-operative Congress voted to set up an Independent Commission to look at reforms and efficiencies to revitalise the movement. Hugh Gaitskell agreed to chair it and asked his protégé, Tony Crosland, to become secretary to the commission. Crosland had been one of those Labour MPs unlucky enough to lose his seat at the 1955 General Election and Gaitskell was keen to put his talents to good use. During 1957 Crosland visited twenty-five co-ops across Britain. With Gaitskell encouraging him to return to parliament, his

---

36   Chain stores like Marks and Spencer and Sainsbury's.

involvement with the co-op led him to seek nomination as a Co-operative MP. Crosland's widow recounts in her memoir of her husband that unfortunately he only 'officially joined the Co-operative Party three weeks before appearing as their nominee before the selection committee. Ian Mikardo wrote in *Tribune* that it was scandalous'.[37] Crosland was beaten by a former pharmaceutical chemist named Alan Brown, the chair of the South Tottenham Co-operative Society.

In February 1957 the Co-operative Party won the nomination for the safe parliamentary seat of Wednesbury for John Stonehouse, a dynamic thirty-two year-old co-op activist who, within a couple of years, was elected as the unusually young president of the London Co-operative Society. His defeat of TSSA[38] president Ray Gunter caused the pent-up resentment of Labour's anti-cooperative elements to boil over, and Labour terminated its electoral agreement with the Co-operative Party pending renegotiation.

The pot had been stirred some more by Gaitskell's great rival Harold Wilson, who had been chairing his own commission (created by the Labour Party in the wake of its poor showing at the 1955 election) on Labour Party organisation. The Wilson Commission is now chiefly remembered for its description of Labour campaigning effectiveness as being 'still at the penny-farthing stage in a jet-propelled era'. Amongst helpful remedies, it eyed the resources of local co-operative societies and urged that they affiliate directly to the Labour Party.[39] The Co-operative Party understandably rejected this as an attempt both to requisition Co-operative Party finance and personnel and also to subsume its distinctive political voice.

Wilson's mischief-making could be weathered so long as Gaitskell remained friendly but a literal 'storm in an egg-cup', as it became known, tipped the balance. The failure of Labour MPs to oppose the Conservative government's Egg Marketing Scheme proposals during the 1955-56 parliamentary session caused Co-operative MPs, who voted against the proposals, to thereby break ranks with Labour in parliament. While the Co-operative Party National Secretary, Jack Bailey, insisted that they had an agreement to differ,[40] Gaitskell told Bailey that he was concerned that the Co-operative Party could be 'a party within a party,' an issue to which Gaitskell had become acutely sensitised following the 'Bevanite' battles of the immediately preceding years. Labour's

---

37   Susan Crosland, *Tony Crosland*, (Jonathan Cape, 1982), p 88

38   Transport Salaried Staffs Association – the main white-collar railway union.

39   The Royal Arsenal Co-operative Society (RACS) in Woolwich (which had once sponsored Herbert Morrison) provided the precedent for this. Uniquely amongst co-operative societies it affiliated to the Labour Party directly. Other co-operative societies affiliated to the Co-operative Party instead.

40   Clause 2 of the 1946 agreement.

suspension of its electoral agreement with the Co-operative Party in 1957 was motivated therefore by resentment at the Co-operative Party's disproportionate success in winning parliamentary selections, a desire to secure direct access for the Labour Party to co-operative finance and Hugh Gaitskell's fear that the independent behaviour of the Co-operative Party would set a dangerous precedent for wider dissent.

Left-wing activists in both Labour and Co-operative parties were increasingly challenging Britain's role in NATO and demanding the unilateral abandonment of atomic weapons. Stan Newens' history of the London Co-operative Society (LCS) recounts that during their 1952 conference, a 'resolution calling for a cut in the rearmament programme was moved from the floor by a young Jim Mortimer and carried by a large majority, despite opposition from Ashley Bramall representing the old guard'.[41]

At the 1954 Co-operative Party conference the MP for East Ham South, Percy Daines, had found himself forced to make a forthright defence of the Party's support for Britain's membership of NATO:

> *'All the [opposing] speakers... are agreed on the pacific intentions of the Russians in all their operations. Appeals like that made by the last speaker to a sort of inverted jingoism... our distaste for America and what she has not done will not help us, because it is a historic fact that the British Labour government with Ernest Bevin as Foreign Secretary gave the warning and took the initial steps to call the attention of the world to the militaristic intentions of the Russians and he did that twelve months before the Americans turned round.'*[42]

Within a few years the LCS political committee would be a leading cheerleader for CND. It was a policy position that in 1960 gained the temporary support of the national Co-operative Party conference, as it did that of the Labour Party as a whole, precipitating Gaitskell's famous pledge to 'fight and fight and fight again.' While during the late 1950s Gaitskell still believed he could handle the challenge from the Labour Party left-wing, he feared the

---

41   Stan Newens, *Working Together, a short history of the London Co-op Society Political Committee* (CRS London political committee, 1988), p 26. Mortimer was in later years the General Secretary of the Labour Party during the 1983 General Election debacle. Bramall, whose brother Edwin became Field Marshall Lord Bramall, was then the thirty-six year-old recently defeated Labour MP for Bexley. Subsequently he would become chairman of the GLC and leader of the Inner London Education Authority (ILEA).

42   Co-op Party conference report 1954, pp 78-79

consequences of pro-Soviet activists gaining control of the Co-operative Party and using it to subvert his leadership of the Labour Party.

The renegotiation of the electoral agreement was tortuous. Labour initially demanded a cap of no more than six Co-operative Party MPs. Ultimately, both sides knew that failure to reach a new agreement would have damaged them both. When a new agreement was finally reached in 1958 it capped the number of delegates a Co-operative Party could send to a Constituency Labour Party to five, in order to prevent parliamentary selection meetings being overwhelmed by Co-operative delegates. It also changed the nomenclature of candidates from Co-operative/Labour to Labour/Co-operative. Additionally, it limited the maximum number of Co-operative MPs (and candidates), but at thirty rather than six. This was a number somewhat higher than the Co-operative Party had thus far managed to attain (the record was twenty-three MPs in 1945 and thirty-eight candidates in 1955).

At the 1959 election, sixteen Co-operative MPs were elected (down three). Despite the embarrassment the Conservatives had suffered with the resignation of Prime Minister Anthony Eden over the Suez fiasco in 1957, they gained seats at Labour's expense. In the subsequent soul-searching that convulsed Labour, Gaitskell and his allies questioned the electoral attractiveness of nationalisation and made an abortive attempt to change Labour's commitment to it as enshrined in Clause IV of its constitution. Though they failed to secure a formal change, the impetus provided made Labour more receptive to the ideas of the Co-operative Party. Thus, despite the wrangling over seats in 1958, Co-operative Party Assistant Secretary Harold Campbell could write in the 1960 publication *Co-operation and Social Ownership*:

'More and more people in the Labour movement have recently begun to ask themselves if nationalisation is necessarily the only and the best form of public ownership to be applied in all cases. For many years the Co-operative Party has said that it is not. Its point of view has gone largely unregarded until quite recently.'[43]

The following year, the Labour Party conceded in its *Signposts for the Sixties* policy document that, 'the form of public ownership will, of course, vary wildly. Already we can see it developing in various forms including... co-operative ownership.'

---

43   Harold Campbell, *Co-operation and Social Ownership*, (Co-operative Union, 1960) p 1

CONSUMER'S CHAMPION?

In 1964 the Co-operative MP and former Party research officer Bert Oram observed: 'There is no longer any doubt as to the relevance of [co-operative ideas] to what Labour plans to do.'[44] This was a substantial claim, and reflected the evolution of the Co-operative Party from a purely defensive pressure group. At the heart of the Co-operative Party vision was the role set out by Harold Campbell, who had been Co-operative Party Assistant Secretary since 1946 and finally succeeded Jack Bailey as Secretary in January 1963, in his 1947 pamphlet *Wanting and Working*:

> *'The Co-operative Party advocates the sovereignty of the consumer. It declares that the state should be controlled in the interests of the consumer as a co-operative society is controlled in his interests... it bases its advocacy upon the socialist ground that consumer control is the only true classless control. The consumer interest is all embracing: any other is a limited interest.... The specific role of the co-operative movement in politics is the advocacy of libertarian socialism, based upon the classlessness of consumer sovereignty. In the drive to make as much headway in five years towards a new and planned Britain by the Labour government, much that is kindly and human and liberal (in its wider sense) is in danger of being overlooked.... In the clash of interests apparent in the transition to the new order – the clash between capital and labour – the claim of the consumer to be the only non-sectional and therefore classless or unifying interest, is in danger of being ignored or – when it is heard – not understood.'[45]*

This was not a wholly new vision. The annual report to the 1928 Co-operative Party conference stated: 'By common consent the members of the Co-operative Group are looked to as the custodians of the interest of the consumer.'[46] But Harold Campbell had put it at the heart of his strategy for rejuvenating the Co-operative Party after the battles with Labour to secure the 1958 agreement.

---

44   Bert Oram MP, *Social Ownership in the Sixties*, (Co-operative Union, 1964) p 4

45   Harold Campbell, *Wanting and Working* (Co-operative Party, 1947), pp 6 & 16

46   Annual report, p 11

Like his predecessor, Jack Bailey, Campbell was an idealist. But his initial focus was practical. For Tom Carbery (who knew both), while Bailey had 'something of the mystique (and occasional vagueness) of the visionary, Campbell was more down to earth.'[47] Campbell modernised party structures, [48] organised summer schools, and encouraged Co-operative MPs to exploit parliamentary opportunities more proactively, for example by using private member's bills on issues wider than simply the narrow interests of co-operative societies themselves – notwithstanding the fact that it was a Conservative government in office with a substantial majority.

Thus it was Co-operative Party lobbying that helped deliver the 1961 Consumer Protection Act which extended safety standards for a wide range of goods. Further Co-operative Party initiatives in 1961 and 1964 resulted in the Hire-Purchase Act 1964 which raised the statutory protection limit and provided a three-day cooling off period for purchasers. Co-operative Party pressure contributed to the Weights and Measures Act 1962. Perhaps most dramatically, it was a private member's bill promoted by Co-operative Party MP John Stonehouse, on the suggestion of Party headquarters, that prompted the new Conservative President of the Board of Trade Edward Heath to push through the abolition of Resale Price Maintenance (RPM) in 1964 – a measure that helped establish Heath's reputation as a Tory 'moderniser'. RPM was the system whereby a manufacturer or wholesaler selling goods to a shop could compel the shop to retail the goods at a fixed price. Edward Heath wrote in his memoir: 'The abolition of RPM was a highly controversial measure among some Conservatives... because it would, in the short term at least, hit some small shopkeepers, many of whom were part of the bedrock of our support in the country.' [49]

Already at the 1962 Co-operative Party conference Harold Wilson had declared: 'We have fought for the removal of the higher rate of profits tax on co-operative undertakings and for the removal of the discrimination against co-operative savings... when we want someone to fight for the rights of consumers we turn to your group and ask George Darling.' [50] When Wilson became Prime Minister after the 1964 general election (which saw an increase in the number of Co-operative Party MPs to nineteen) he ensured that he appointed Co-

47   Thomas Carbery, *Consumers in Politics*, (Manchester University Press, 1969), p 52

48   Campbell reduced the burden of internal committees by changing the party national
        executive meetings from monthly to bi-monthly, and eliminating policy and
        organisation sub-committees, using more informal processes as necessary and
        generally shaking the dust of accumulated precedent off the operational apparatus.

49   Edward Heath, *The Course of My Life*, (Hodder & Stoughton, 1998), p 259

50   Wilson was chair of the Labour Party for that year.

operative MPs to portfolios where they could foster particular Co-operative priorities. Chief among these was his decision to give Co-operative MP George Darling responsibility for consumer affairs when he appointed him as Minister of State at the Board of Trade.[51]

Another important appointment was that of Bert Oram, as Barbara Castle's deputy at the new Ministry of Overseas Development. There he was able to build upon the work already being undertaken to foster the development of co-operatives overseas. The one place Conservative governments had been prepared to encouraged co-ops (especially in agriculture) was in Britain's shrinking empire and for many years the Colonial and Commonwealth Relations offices had sponsored African, Caribbean and Asian students at the Co-operative College in Loughborough. On a visit to Tanzania, Oram found a third of the cabinet wearing Co-operative College ties.[52]

Other Co-operative MPs appointed to government included Dickson Mabon as Under-Secretary of State for Scotland and John Stonehouse as Roy Jenkins's deputy at the Ministry of Aviation. Mabon would be promoted to deputy Secretary of State for Scotland from 1967 and Stonehouse, after a stint at the Colonial Office and as Aviation minister, was appointed Britain's last Postmaster-General in 1968.

Lord Beswick, who had served Attlee as junior Civil Aviation minister during 1950-51, was appointed a whip in the Lords.[53] Further promotion came with a stint as Under-Secretary for the Colonies from 1965, and his appointment as government chief whip in the Lords in 1967. Sidney Irving, Co-operative MP for Dartford since 1955 became deputy government chief whip and subsequently deputy speaker.[54] Wilson also appointed the Co-operative MP for Stoke-on-Trent North, Harriet Slater, as a government whip.[55]

---

51   Darling had succeeded AV Alexander as MP for Sheffield Hillsborough on the latter's elevation to the Lords in 1950. He was a former Co-operative Wholesale Society head of research (1930-37) and BBC industrial correspondent (1942-49). He continued as Minister responsible for Consumer Affairs until he retired to the backbenches in 1968 at the age of sixty-two.

52   Carbery, op cit, p 175

53   Frank Beswick had been Co-operative MP for Uxbridge 1945-59. When Labour went in opposition in 1970 he continued as Opposition Chief Whip in the Lords 1970-74. As the only co-operator in the shadow cabinet he was the senior Co-operative Party parliamentarian.

54   Irving was deputy speaker 1966-70. He was defeated at the 1970 General Election.

55   Slater had trained as a teacher in Dudley before working as Co-operative Party national organiser 1942-1953. Elected MP for Stoke-on-Trent North, where she was a local councillor, at a by-election in 1953, she served as a government whip until her retirement from parliament aged sixty-three at the 1966 General Election.

Much of the consumer legislation that the 21st century shopper takes for granted is rooted in the hard work of Co-operative Party MPs during the 1960s Wilson governments. It was George Darling who secured the 1968 Trade Descriptions Act (the 'shoppers charter'). The Co-operative Party MP for Wood Green, Joyce Butler,[56] unsuccessfully promoted a Food Labelling Bill in 1965, but her farm and garden chemicals bill became law in 1968. So too did the Clean Air Bill of her Co-operative MP colleague Bob Edwards, a volunteer for the Republican cause in the Spanish Civil War who during 1937 had served briefly as George Orwell's platoon commander on the Aragon front. Edwards' Council Tenants Charter Bill 1968 and Alf Morris's[57] Housing (Local Authority Contributions) Bill 1969 failed to get through. But a private member's bill proposed by Co-operative MP Tom Williams[58] removing restrictions on off-licences became law. Outside parliament too, the Co-operative Party was agitating as the champion of consumers. The 1966 report of the national committee urged members to 'take an interest in the Consultative Committees of nationalised industries which are not as effective as they might be… to examine public transport, hospitals, pre-natal clinics and the like.' By the early 1970s, future issues were anticipated by resolutions at Co-operative Party conferences on food additives, pollution, and country of origin marks.

Another area the Co-operative Party worked hard to encourage, but where it received less gratitude from the beneficiaries, was in the field of agricultural co-operatives. They had been growing in number since the early 1950s. But many farmers who operated in co-operatives were unwilling to identify with the co-operative movement because of a reluctance to associate themselves with the Labour Party.[59] Nevertheless, the Co-operative Party (making good use of the influence wielded by Co-operative MP Alf Morris as PPS to agriculture minister Fred Peart) helped to secure a 1965 White Paper giving backing for agricultural

---

56   Butler grew up in Birmingham but had led the Labour group on Wood Green council, north London, over many years and been the new Haringey council's first chair. Her husband, a fellow councillor, was the first Mayor of Haringey.

57   Morris, who had a degree in history from Oxford despite leaving school at fourteen to become a clerk, had become MP for Manchester Wythenshaw in 1964. He and his elder brother Charles (father of Tony Blair's cabinet minister Estelle) would serve as ministers in subsequent Wilson governments.

58   A Welsh barrister and Baptist minister. Williams was MP for Hammersmith South from a 1949 by-election to 1955, Baron's Court from 1955 to 1959, and Warrington from a 1961 by-election. He served as a PPS to several ministers and became a QC in 1964. In 1981 he was appointed a judge.

59   Although a few affiliated to the Co-operative Union.

co-operatives.[60] The subsequent Bill went through the Commons in 1967. It established a new scheme administered by a new Central Council for Agriculture and Horticulture Co-operation[61] with a budget to organise and promote co-operation within agriculture and horticulture.

60   *Guardian* 5 April 1965

61   On which the co-operative movement had statutory representation.

TAXING TIMES

Despite the very real impact of its activities in Parliament, the Co-operative Party was not as successful as it had hoped in securing recognition amongst the wider public for its achievements as the consumer's champion. As Professor Sidney Pollard observed in his study *The Co-operatives at the Crossroads*, such was the link between the Co-operative Party and the Co-operative Movement, as represented in the public mind by its retail arm, that:

> *'This objective... [of becoming the consumers' champion in politics] can only be carried out if co-operative shops are the leaders and the standard-bearers in respect of the quality of their commodities and in the surroundings in which they are sold. The interests of members and the place of the co-operative movement in society demand that the service provided in their own shops should raise the dignity of the co-operative shopper.'[62]*

Unfortunately this was not always the case. The credibility of the Co-operative Party's push for consumer rights was undermined by an insufficient sensitivity to consumer preferences in too many co-op shops. Tom Carbery, whose history of the Co-operative Party was published in 1969, quotes a contemporary Labour MP whose sympathy clearly lay with the Party's plight: 'The Co-operative Party's observations on consumer affairs are spot-on and deserve to be pushed – if only they did not have to carry the co-operative movement around with them like [George] Lansbury's conscience.'[63] For Carbery: '...most folk are not over-inspired by co-operative service. Too often... the local retail society is equated with dowdiness and uninspiring sales service. It is not long since a national daily described the average Co-operative shop window as being reminiscent of that of a shop in a suburb of Kharkov. To many a working-class mother it is St Michael who is the patron saint of the consumer.'[64]

The co-operative movement was sufficiently aware of the challenge presented by the likes of Marks and Spencer that it had become the butt of conference humour. At the St Andrews Co-operative Party Summer School in

---

62   Prof Sidney Pollard, *The co-operatives at the crossroads*, (Fabian Research Series No. 245), p 14

63   Carbery, *op cit*, p 211

64   Carbery, *op cit*, p 210

1964, the gossip sheet had a story of Party chair Lord Peddie dying and going to heaven only to be confronted with a tall, dignified figure who introduced himself as St Michael. 'My God,' said Peddie, 'don't tell me Marks has got in here as well.'[65]

The problems were certainly very real. Elected in 1956 at the age of thirty-one to the management board of the London Co-operative Society, the largest co-op in the country, John Stonehouse found himself 'the youngest Director by over twenty years, and the only one who was not an elderly housewife or an employee.... I was an odd man out and made to feel it.'[66] At that time the London Co-operative Society (LCS) had fourteen hundred shops, the biggest dairy service in London, a dozen department stores and a substantial funeral service. The LCS membership had peaked in 1951 and by 1962 would decline below 1945 levels. Stan Newens recounts in his history of the LCS political committee that in the 1940s 'the LCS was still the dominant retailer in its trading area and 40% of households included a member; still more were consumers of products bought at co-op shops,' but that by the early 1950s, 'the LCS was ... stalling in terms of trading prowess. Despite the fact that it was a pioneer of self-service, its commitment to a policy of a co-op shop on every corner caused it to lag behind in the transformation which was beginning to overtake the retail trade... private traders began to seem more modern and more attractive to many of those who were benefiting from the new affluence.'[67] For Stonehouse: 'It had the sinews of strength if only it would stretch its muscles,' but 'the loyalty of members was being eroded by the sheer facts of bad service, poor merchandising and sometimes higher prices.'[68]

The very success of the co-op over so many decades made it all the more resistant to change. So affluent had the Scottish Co-operative Wholesale Society once been that it had chosen the runner-up from the architectural competition for Glasgow City Hall as the design for its own headquarters on the banks of the Clyde. Recognising the reality of decline was too painful an ordeal for some to face. Former Co-operative MP Lord Foulkes recalls: 'Many local societies were too reluctant to agree mergers because people on the boards didn't want to lose their positions.'[69]

The failure of the Co-operative retail and wholesale arm to become a beacon of consumer responsiveness was highlighted by the report of the Co-operative Independent Commission (the 'Gaitskell Commission'), which Tony Crosland

65   Carbery, *op cit,* p 210

66   John Stonehouse, *Death of an Idealist,* (W H Allen, 1975), p 32

67   Newens, *op cit,* p 24-25

68   Stonehouse, *op cit,* p 34 and p 32

69   Lord Foulkes, interview with the author.

had written during 1957-58. In an essay originally published in 1961[70] Crosland
wrote that co-operation:

> *'Provides the additional benefits, much to be valued in our centralised,
> bureaucratic and producer-dominated society, of local autonomy,
> member participation and consumer control. Unfortunately, despite
> brilliant successes in some spheres (such as self-service) and some
> localities (Nottingham, Portsmouth, Bristol)... its share of retail trade,
> after stagnating at about 11% for the past 25 years, has now begun to
> decline; and it has been markedly less successful than the multiples in
> adapting to the consumer revolution of the last decade... The main
> weakness is... in the supposed interests of "equality and democracy", the
> Movement pays absurdly low salaries, recruits few university or even
> grammar school personnel, permits excessive interference with
> management by elected lay Boards, and above all displays an intense
> hostility to strong, professional, national leadership. The result (with
> some notable exceptions) is a certain dowdiness, parochialism, and
> technical backwardness; and this, far from fostering equality or
> democracy, merely reduces the Co-operative share of activity, and hence
> the area over which Co-operative principles can be applied... If the
> Movement could overcome these weaknesses...[it could]... provide a
> splendid example of competitive social enterprise and a much-needed
> countervailing power to producer interests.'[71]*

But it didn't, despite the report Crosland had written for the Gaitskell
Commission. Nor, despite his urging, did it exploit the opportunities to move
into new areas: to challenge the petrol distribution network of the large oil
companies or (in those days before ITV) to create a viable co-operative
alternative to the BBC television monopoly.

Instead, the recommendations of the Gaitskell Commission were subjected to
fresh conferences and working groups until, as John Stonehouse recalled in his
memoir, they were 'buried under a welter of talk and paper'. Dick Marsh, who
would serve alongside Crosland as a Cabinet minister in the 1960s Wilson
governments, had been a Co-operative Party candidate in 1951 and, until his
election as MP for Greenwich in 1959, had been one of those seeking to coax
the co-operative movement into implementing the Gaitskell Commission's
recommendations. In his memoir he recalls: 'I joined, for my sins, a Rules

---

70   Included in the volume of essays he published the following year entitled *The
        Conservative Enemy.*

71   Anthony Crosland, *The Conservative Enemy*, (Jonathan Cape, 1962), p 45-46

Revision Committee of the Royal Arsenal Co-operative Society, the largest co-operative in the country, to implement the recommendations of the Crosland Report. After two years of work, we made something like 180 recommendations, and I had the satisfaction of watching every single one of them voted down by the membership, whose desire for revolutionary change was theoretical rather than practical.'[72] As the Co-operative Party chair Lord Peddie said in his chair's address to the 1962 Co-operative Party conference: 'Too many persuade themselves that they are defending democratic rights when they are in fact protecting vested interests. There are others who believe the employment of modern techniques of management and closer co-ordination of wholesale and retail functions are a challenge to traditional principles. This need not be so.'

Belated action was taken during the 1960s. In 1966 a regional plan, promoted by the Co-operative Union, sought the amalgamation of the then six hundred and eighty societies into fifty-five regional societies. The same year the Co-operative Wholesale Society appointed its first 'outsider' chief executive, Philip Thomas. Tragically he was killed in a plane crash less than two years later, before the programme of radical change he introduced could come to fruition. Some elements were immediately visible. Operation 'Facelift' in 1968 entailed the introduction of the first national 'Co-op' logo.

But just as the movement seemed to be making progress, like the Wilson government itself, it was blown off course. In 1965 the Co-operative Permanent Building Society, the third-largest society in the country, was successfully expanding. It operated as agents for the CWS who in turn appointed two of its full-time directors. During a 1969 BBC TV *Nationwide* programme on the collapse of the Millom co-operative society in Cumbria, a senior co-operative figure unwisely said that there could be no assurance that other societies would not close. This led to a run on deposits at the Co-operative Permanent Building Society because of its 'Co-operative' name. The board needed little further convincing to change it to 'Nationwide'. By the late 1980s, having merged with 'Anglia', the Nationwide Anglia had assets of more than eighteen billion pounds, five and a half million savers and eight hundred and fifty thousand mortgage borrowers. It became the world's largest mutual building society after it refused to follow the example of many of its rivals and become a bank. But because it had dropped the word 'Co-operative' from its name it was no longer associated in the public mind with the co-operative movement.

Meanwhile the Co-operative Party in parliament was wrestling with another setback: the introduction by Harold Wilson's Chancellor of the Exchequer, Jim Callaghan, of a new Selective Employment Tax (SET) in the May 1966 Budget. Callaghan needed to raise revenue but Wilson had asked him to help his mission to present Labour as a 'modernising' government by finding a new and more imaginative way to raise revenue than by simply raising income tax. With the assistance of his Special Advisor, Cambridge University economist Nicholas Kaldor, Callaghan came up with SET. As he explained to the Commons it aimed, 'at one and the same time to tax the employment in services and construction but lessen the cost of employment in manufacturing.'[73] It was certainly innovative, but, if anything, it was regressive; penalising employment in new service industries to lessen the burden on the UK's overmanned traditional manufacturing sector which had above all to automate and mechanise in order to survive. As David Wise[74] told Tom Carbery: 'The Co-operative Party was right. But being right is no longer a virtue in the Labour Movement.'[75]

SET was welcomed by the powerful manufacturing trade unions, who wanted at all costs to preserve manufacturing jobs. It gave a 130% rebate – effectively a subsidy – to manufacturing industry. The introduction of SET came on top of a series of impositions on consumers: an increase in national insurance rates; in postal charges, in motor tax, in rating assessments; and the soon-to-be-implemented Industrial Training Board levy. Co-operative Party MPs recognised its impact on the co-operative retail sector and immediately raised concerns in the House of Commons. Laurie Pavitt, protested that, 'the new tax… is likely to have an immediate effect on prices. Once again it is the housewife who will have to bear the burden…. I estimate that this new kind of tax might well eliminate the dividend in some societies…'[76] Co-operative MPs Alf Morris and Tom Williams raised similar concerns. 'It's the only boat I've got,' Callaghan is reported to have said. 'Help me push it out. We can change the superstructure later.'[77]

Some Co-operative MPs talked of open rebellion - but when the division bell rang they loyally supported the government. Co-operative MPs were constrained by the discipline of the Parliamentary Labour Party under the terms of the 1958 agreement. *Co-operative News* reported the attitude of Co-operative MPs as 'Aye Vote Now – Battle Later'[78] Nevertheless, grassroots co-operative activists condemned MPs for not doing enough. MP Geoffrey Rhodes wrote in the 21 May edition of *Co-operative News*: 'What does the co-op movement want – an explosion of emotion and a lobby rebellion… or does it want results in the form

---

73   James Callaghan, Hansard 3 May 1966

74   Co-operative Party research officer. Wise was subsequent Co-operative Party National
       Secretary 1974-92.

75   David Wise verbatim note taken by Thomas Carbery cited Carbery, *op cit,* p 235

76   Laurie Pavitt MP, Hansard 3 May 1966.

77   James Callaghan cited Carbery, *op cit,* p 225

78   *Co-operative News* headline 14 May 1966

of specific concessions? The two are probably mutually exclusive. Our only hope of winning the day on this issue is not so much in terms of our numbers – which are small – but in our personal influence and goodwill amongst our Labour colleagues.'[79]

It was in the midst of this storm that Harold Campbell stepped down as party secretary to become deputy chairman of the Housing Corporation. Co-operative housing had been the subject of Campbell's first pamphlet and this was an opportunity for him to promote his ideas in practice. His successor, Ted Graham, was the Southern Sectional Secretary of the Co-operative Union. Graham was already a Co-operative Party veteran, having joined the Newcastle-upon-Tyne Co-operative Party in 1942 aged seventeen and, like Campbell, he had been a leading light in the British Federation of Young Co-operators.[80] Graham had continued his political activities alongside his involvement in the co-operative movement: he had been leader of Enfield Council since 1962 and had stood against Iain MacLeod at the 1966 general election. Like both Jack Bailey and Harold Campbell he was an activist in the Enfield Highway Co-operative Society (based on the armaments works that had made the famous Lee Enfield rifle of the World Wars).

If anyone was suited to coping with the vicissitudes of the time it was Graham. As a child he had survived a vicious knife attack by local boys out to steal the Graham family shopping. As a young man he endured friendly-fire injuries' from a comrade's Bren-gun whilst in training as a Royal Marine Commando for the D-Day landings.[81] His warmth, infectious enthusiasm and understated modesty was rooted in his upbringing on the Scotswood Road in Tyneside. Graham had passed the eleven-plus but left school at fourteen to become an errand boy at the Newcastle Co-op. In 1976 he would become the first MP to gain a degree from the Open University and he remains the only MP to have done so while actually serving in parliament.[82] His cousin Miriam (who married playwright Tom Stoppard) recalled: 'In the Geordie family whose political history had always been socialist my cousin Lord Ted of Ed [as he later became] was the unequivocal star, although it was not until I was quite grown up that I understood the strength of his candlepower.'

Hardly had Graham settled in than the SET row flared up once more. Roy Jenkins, who replaced Callaghan as Chancellor of the Exchequer in November 1967 threatened to raise it further and at the 1968 Co-operative Party conference

---

79   Geoffrey Rhodes MP, *Co-operative News* 21 May 1966, p 2

80   Graham had been national secretary of the BFYC 1952-53. His involvement in youth politics also included a stint as prime minister of the Tyneside Youth Parliament.

81   Lord Graham, *From Tyne to Thames,* (The Memoir Club, 2005), p 22. He wrote 'not many people can say that they have held their guts in their hands but I can.'

82   He did most of his studying on the Victoria Line tube.

Graham had to face down calls for Co-operative MPs to vote against the Labour Government. Graham declared: 'We are told that if we do not pass this amendment it will destroy the movement. We are told that if we do pass the amendment we shall destroy the party.'[83] The amendment was substantially defeated on a show of hands. Moreover, concessions were eventually secured by Co-operative MPs from government: the Ministry of Agriculture (where Co-operative MP Alf Morris was PPS) agreed to allow 90% of the cost of SET as an expense in the calculation of costs and profits on distribution of milk. This saved the co-op some £1.3m from the total SET bill of £9.5m.

Securing the abolition of SET was hampered by a deeper problem, namely that the Co-operative Party's opposition to SET was not underpinned by a coherent alternative tax policy. If SET were abolished, the Co-operative Party were unable to articulate where the replacement revenue would come from. This undermined the credibility of its critique, prescient though it was.

Battered by rows over spending cuts and Barbara Castle's abortive plan to reform industrial relations, Harold Wilson's government nevertheless anticipated victory at the 1970 general election.[84] However bad things had been, Edward Heath's Conservative Party lacked credibility. But the unexpected happened. Heath won and the Co-operative Party shared Labour's defeat. Several Co-operative MPs lost their seats including both Sydney Irving[85] and Ioan Evans[86] Ironically it was the new Conservative government that would finally lance the boil of SET by abolishing it altogether, making up the revenue through a mixture of spending cuts that included Mrs Thatcher's famous snatching of free school milk and the introduction of VAT.

---

83   Verbatim notes of Graham speech cited Carbery, *op cit,* p 233

84   *In Place of Strife.*

85   Irving was MP for Dartford since 1955, had served as government deputy chief whip 1964-66 and had been Deputy Speaker of the Commons since 1966.

86   Evans had been MP for Birmingham Yardley since 1964 and a senior government whip since 1966.

THEMES FOR THE SEVENTIES

The battered Co-operative Party needed rejuvenation following the fall of the Wilson government. Graham knew that to turn Co-operative dreams into reality the party needed a deeper working relationship with the Labour Party. To achieve it, he organised events that brought Labour MPs and ministers together with the co-operative societies in their areas, organised delegations from co-operative societies to meet ministers at Westminster, and arranged regional events with joint panels from the 'trinity of the labour movement': the Co-operative Party, the Labour Party and the trade unions. 'The period was not a good one for the government or for the Labour Party in general,' Ted Graham recalls, 'the meetings attracted a fair number of disgruntled people, but it was seen to be an attempt to demonstrate that from our point of view we were part of that trinity of the working-class [and that] the Co-operative arm was alive and kicking and ready to play a full part in securing a Labour government.'[87] Behind the scenes Graham worked hard to cement relations with Terry Pitt, who had replaced Peter Shore as head of research at Labour head-office in 1965. They forged a quietly effective partnership.

Graham sought firstly to build on the Co-operative Party's record as the voice of consumers (and George Darling's record in office as consumer affairs minister within the department of trade), by securing a commitment from a future Labour government to create a ministry for consumer affairs. This had been Co-operative Party policy since 1954 but Labour had not yet been convinced. Secondly, he sought a Labour pledge to establish a Co-operative Development Agency – in essence a co-op equivalent of the Industrial Re-organisation Corporation[88] – intended to promote new producer co-operatives and encourage the rationalisation and modernisation of existing co-operatives. Thirdly, Graham sought reassurance that a future Labour government would take action to promote co-operative housing schemes as an alternative to the municipal and private sectors.

Graham's agenda was reflected in a major speech by Tony Crosland, who

---

87   Lord Graham. Letter to the author.

88   Created in 1966 by the by the Frank Cousins/ Tony Benn Ministry of Technology to foster mergers and efficiencies in the private sector. It was abolished by Heath's Conservative government.

had been invited to address the April 1971 Co-operative Party annual conference as a special guest. His speech was published by the Party as a pamphlet that same year entitled *A Critical commentary on Co-operative Progress*.

It was more than a decade since the co-operative movement had failed to embrace the recommendations of the report he had written for the Gaitskell Commission. Crosland, now a senior member of Wilson's shadow cabinet, took the opportunity to remind his audience that he had 'spent the best years of my life working with and for the [co-op] movement... I... acquired a strong loyalty to the British co-op movement that reflects itself not only in my shopping habits.' He was not shy to emphasise that customer habit would be insufficient to sustain them in the future, highlighting the 'appalling fact... that from 1957 to 1970 the co-operative share of trade has fallen by almost a third – from 11.9% to under 8%... [although it] has retained 15% of national grocery trade.' He urged a move to better store locations, a national co-op brand image, 'the employment of the best managerial brains at competitive salaries,'[89] and the expansion of the co-op into travel, motor trades and housing. 'The movement will never succeed by trying to be merely a second Marks and Spencer or a second Sainsbury's. All it would achieve would be a poor imitation. We have to establish ourselves as a good business with a difference.'[90]

It would take more than a decade for Crosland's business advice to the co-operative retail movement to bear fruit. This would continue to hamper the effectiveness of the Co-operative Party as the political wing of the movement. As Ted Graham recalled in his memoir: 'The credibility of the Co-operative case was in direct proportion to its standing in the marketplace or on the High Street. At that time it was an uphill struggle.'[91]

Politically, he was more upbeat. Taking Graham's three themes in turn, Crosland sought to put them at the heart of a partnership between the Co-operative Party and the next Labour government. On consumer protection he declared: 'I am a firm believer in competition. But by itself it is certainly not enough. For one thing, we live not in a 19th Century world of small firms, but in a world of huge semi-monopolistic giants which are often immune from the full rigours of competition...' He advocated a reconstituted and stronger Consumer Council (recently abolished by the Conservatives) to ensure the effective enforcement of legislation; an advisory service on consumer rights; a small claims court to enable cheap prosecution of defaulting suppliers; a strengthened scrutiny of monopolies and mergers 'to make competition more

---

89   An objective agreed in principle by the Co-operative Union and Labour's NEC in 1970.

90   Anthony Crosland, *A Critical commentary on Co-operative Progress*, (Co-operative Party 1971), p 4

91   Lord Graham, *From Tyne to Thames via the usual channels* (The Memoir Club, 2005), p 19

effective' and a renewed attempt at prices and incomes policy.

On co-operative housing he emphasised the need to tackle the capital shortage which hampered the growth of housing co-operatives: 'We believe that people should be able to live in a community, yet at the same time be able to participate democratically in running that community. Neither owner-occupation nor municipal ownership provide this possibility. Co-operative housing does.'

Endorsing the proposed Co-operative Development Agency, he emphasised its role 'to act as a merger-broker and to provide loan capital – functions very similar to those of the IRC. It would in no sense seek to prop up inefficiency. The object would be to aid and galvanise a socially important form of enterprise.'[92]

The three policy themes would be reflected in Labour's commitments at the next election. It would take a few more years for a Labour government to take on board some of the other issues raised by the Co-operative Party at that time. At the 1972 annual conference they included equalising the age of retirement at sixty for both men and women; grants to encourage school attendance from sixteen to eighteen; and longer statutory holidays. A further issue for the Co-operative Party was one with which Labour was notably reluctant to engage: the failings of the great nationalised industries. In March 1971 the Co-operative Party had given evidence to the inquiry of the Parliamentary Select Committee on the nationalised industries into relations between the industries and the public. It argued that consumer representation was inadequate and urged that a more powerful consumer voice be set up. Alf Morris MP, the chair of the Co-operative MPs during 1972, raised it directly in his conference speech that year:

'In most of the giant statutory, commercial, industrial and other organisations of our time, individual people are made to feel increasingly powerless. They see themselves as prisoners of an impersonal and bureaucratic, but above all soulless machine. Many individuals... felt themselves to be on the receiving end of decisions that they have done nothing to influence and can do nothing to change... Unless the organisations which control the quality of their lives can reform themselves, by becoming more accountable to ordinary people, they may well increasingly reject these organisations. For they will not forever accept a largely self-appointed and self-perpetuating leadership that attempts to dehumanise people by its insensitive and ruthless decisions...'[93]

---

92   Anthony Crosland, *A Critical commentary on Co-operative Progress*, (Co-operative Party 1971), pp 6-8

93   Alf Morris, Chair Parliamentary Co-operative group, address to Co-operative Congress at Scarborough, May 1972, pp 7-10

The inability of his government to solve the miners' strike of the winter 1973-74 prompted Prime Minister Edward Heath to call an election for February 1974 on the issue of 'Who runs Britain'. The answer came back: 'not you'. The Conservative vote fell to 38% and though marginally ahead of Labour in the ballot boxes the first-past-the-post electoral system meant that Heath had four fewer MPs than the combined Labour and Co-operative Parties. The Liberal Party secured 19% of the vote, their best since 1929 and fourteen seats, their highest tally since 1935. After the Liberals refused to join a Tory coalition under Heath, Wilson formed a minority Labour government. The Co-operative Party, with sixteen seats, was the third largest party in the Commons and a vital part of the parliamentary arithmetic. It included amongst its number several talented younger MPs with ministerial potential: John Roper at Farnworth, Ian Wrigglesworth at Teeside, Jim Craigen at Glasgow Maryhill and Ted Graham himself, who was elected for Edmonton. Graham's successor as national secretary was David Wise who had been assistant secretary since 1967 and had been research officer before that. Wise was the first Party Secretary since Sam Perry not to have a link with Enfield. Instead his base was Dartford, where he had been leader of the Labour group on the Borough Council and President of the Invicta Co-operative Society.[94]

One of his first challenges was presented by the sudden death aged forty-five of MP Geoffrey Rhodes.[95] Wise moved fast to help secure the nomination for another Co-operative candidate – in this case Mike Thomas, who had been research officer at Party headquarters during the late 1960s – who fortunately held the seat at the by-election.

A major issue for Wise was the lack of a senior Co-operative MP in Wilson's new government at a senior level. Lord Beswick[96] was appointed Minister of State for Industry and was the most senior Co-operative parliamentarian in the government. Among Co-operative MPs, Alf Morris was appointed junior minister

---

94   The name 'Invicta' is the historic motto of Kent – 'undefeated' by William the Conqueror.

95   Co-operative MP for Newcastle East since 1964, Rhodes was a former lecturer in business studies and president of Leeds University Union. He had been another of the potential talents of the party.

96   Frank Beswick was Co-operative Party MP for Uxbridge 1945-59, serving as PPS to the Minister for Air 1946-49 and UK observer at Bikini atomic bomb tests 1946. He was a junior minister at Ministry of Civil Aviation 1950-51. Created a peer by Wilson in 1964 he had served as a whip 1964-65, as junior minister at the Colonies and Commonwealth offices 1965-67 and as Government and then Opposition Chief Whip in the Lords 1967-74

at the Ministry of Health and Social Services, with special responsibility for the disabled. Influenced by the suffering of his father, who had been gassed by the Germans on the Western Front during the First World War, Morris had made a name for himself as a campaigner on disabled issues. Most notably he had secured the Chronically Sick and Disabled Persons Act as a private member in 1970. The other appointments to government were of Laurie Pavitt MP[97] and Lord Jacques[98] – both to the whips office. Several new MPs were appointed PPS to ministers: Jim Craigen to Scottish Secretary Willie Ross, Ted Graham to consumer affairs minister Alan Williams and Ian Wrigglesworth to Home Office minister Alex Lyon (for six months) and then to Home Secretary Roy Jenkins.

Of the senior figures from the 1960s, George Darling and Bert Oram had retired from the Commons.[99] With two major exceptions the other Co-operative MPs were either talented but too young and inexperienced for ministerial office (such as Graham, Roper, Wrigglesworth, Craigen and Thomas), past their best (Joyce Butler, Arthur Palmer, Tom Williams, Sydney Irving and Ioan Evans), or too far to the left for inclusion in the government (Bob Edwards and Stan Newens). The two remaining MPs (Dickson Mabon and John Stonehouse) were the first Co-operative MPs since AV Alexander who were seen as potential senior cabinet material. For two very different reasons Wilson gave neither a government role.

Mabon's ministerial chief from 1964-70 had been Wilson's dour Secretary of State for Scotland: Willie Ross. Since 1967 he had been Ross's deputy, remaining so when, in 1970, Labour went into Opposition. For Tom Carbery, Mabon was 'the best Secretary of State for Scotland we never had and could have been a good PM.' Ross undoubtedly regarded Mabon as his chief political rival. Fellow Co-operative MP Jim Craigen recalls Mabon telling him: 'The trouble with Willie is not who he likes but who he least dislikes.' Ross resented both Mabon's sureness of touch with the media and his policy enthusiasms: while Ross was a Wilson trusty, anti-devolution and euro-sceptic, Mabon was not only a Gaitskellite but was both pro-devolution and pro-EEC. It was his enthusiasm for the EEC that would fatally damage his relations with Wilson. 'Dick had

---

97   Pavitt had been MP for Willseden West since 1959. Like Ted Graham, Pavitt had been National Secretary of the British Federation of Young Co-operators (1941-46) and was a former Education Officer of the Co-operative Union (1947-52).

98   Jacques was a miner's son who had been the highly regarded Chief Executive of the Portsea Island Co-op in Portsmouth from 1945 until his elevation to the chairmanship of the Co-operative Union in 1964. Wilson had been sufficiently impressed to create him a peer in 1968.

99   The former on grounds of age and the latter following the abolition of his constituency by the Boundary Commission.

enthusiasm and he had ideas and he would push them,' fellow Co-operative MP Jim Craigen recalls. His pro-European enthusiasms and skill as a debater put him at the forefront of the great European rebellion of 1971 when sixty-nine Labour and Co-operative MPs including Roy Jenkins, Roy Hattersley, John Smith, Bill Rodgers and Shirley Williams defied the Labour whip to vote for Britain's entry into the EEC (which at the previous election Labour had supported). Like Jenkins, Mabon resigned from the front-bench. Instinctively courageous, the resignation letter he sent to Wilson was nothing if not direct. Wilson never forgave him and the enmity of both Ross (on whom Wilson heavily relied) and now Wilson himself proved career-limiting. While Wilson remained leader, Mabon would not be in his government. Although he made himself busy on the backbenches, he was therefore unable to perform the 'Mr Co-op' role within Government that the Party needed most.[100]

If Mabon's absence from government was a set-back for the Co-operative Party, Stonehouse's was fortuitous. A decade before, Stonehouse had been a golden boy of the co-operative movement. Harold Wilson had even lent Stonehouse and his family his holiday bungalow on the Scilly Isles. Since 1970 he had spent his time as a backbench MP trying to make a success of the British-Bangladeshi bank he had founded. Spiralling debts precipitated events which culminated with his disappearance off a Miami beach on 21 November 1974. His apparent suicide followed a succession of Tory sex scandals and fed into the media furore over the disappearance of Lord Lucan on 8 November 1974, following the murder of his children's nanny. A month later, Australian police arrested a man they believed to be Lucan who turned out, in fact, to be Stonehouse. He had faked his own death and fled to Australia with his mistress under an assumed name. His extradition to face trial in the UK and subsequent conviction for theft and false pretences created a media sensation.

David Wise kept the Co-operative Party as far away from the political fallout around Stonehouse as possible[101] and sought to build on the relationships forged during Ted Graham's tenure as Party Secretary to ensure that in spite of the inclement political weather the Co-operative Party partnership with Labour bore fruit.

The first tangible achievement came immediately after Wilson announced his

---

100   Interviews with Tom Carbery, Jim Craigen, George Foulkes. 'Willie Ross' by Tam Dalyell in *Dictionary of Labour Biography*, by Greg Rosen (ed), (Politicos, 2001). Mabon served simultaneously as chair of the Scottish Parliamentary Labour Party (1975-76), of the Labour Committee for Europe (1974-76), of the cross-party European Movement during the 1975 EEC referendum campaign. He was also the first chair of the moderate Manifesto Group of Labour MPs 1974-76) which he co-founded as a moderate counterbalance to the left-wing Tribune Group.

101   When Stonehouse was sent to prison in 1976 the Conservatives would win the seat with a substantial majority.

government. Though he failed to appoint any Co-operative MPs to it as ministers, Wilson created a Ministry of Consumer Affairs, one of the Co-operative Party aspirations. Shirley Williams was to lead it, with the title of Secretary of State for Prices and Consumer Protection. Her deputy, Alan Williams, would appoint Ted Graham as his PPS.[102] Such was the economic climate, the Ministry spent more of its time wrestling with prices (inflation hit 26% in early 1975) than thinking creatively about consumer issues. When Margaret Thatcher came to power at the 1979 election she abolished it, relegating consumer affairs to a junior ministerial role within the DTI. Nevertheless, while it lasted, its very existence was a Co-operative Party achievement.

The second achievement concerned co-operative housing. Harold Campbell, Ted Graham's predecessor as Party Secretary, had gone to the Housing Corporation largely in order to further the cause of co-operative housing as a 'third way' between municipal social housing and the private rented sector. Several housing ministers in the 1960s Wilson governments had been keen to promote co-operative housing (notably Tony Greenwood, Minister for Housing in Cabinet from 1966, and Dick Mabon who had been responsible for housing at the Scottish Office). Harold Campbell had toured Britain during the late 1950s encouraging local authorities to make land available to co-op housing societies. Some had been launched in the Midlands and South; but not many. The reluctance of municipal Labour groups to consider the merits of co-operative housing was stifling. Without the support of municipal authorities it proved difficult to get schemes going, despite the endorsement of Tony Benn, who declared in an address to the 1972 Co-operative Party conference: 'Co-operative housing makes the householder a self-manager and not just a name in a rent-book...' [103]

The impasse was finally broken in 1974 by Reg Freeson (Labour MP for Willesden East since 1964).[104] Though not a Co-operative MP, he had been a Co-operative Party member since 1958 and had known and admired Harold Campbell and Ted Graham from their days as north London councillors. Appointed junior housing minister by Wilson in 1969 his tenure had been

---

102   The junior minister was a young Scottish Labour MP Robert Maclennan. Williams was
        succeeded by Roy Hattersley in 1976 and Alan Williams was replaced by John Fraser.
        Maclennan remained in post 1974-79.

103   Tony Benn address to 1972 Co-operative Party conference, p 4

104   Freeson had been raised in a Jewish orphanage in West Norwood after being
        abandoned by his parents at the age of five. After war service he had become a
        (largely self-taught) journalist. He had joined Labour in 1948 and the Co-operative
        Party in 1958. He served as leader first of Willesden council and then of its successor
        Brent 1958-65.

curtailed after eight months by the defeat of the Government at the General Election. He continued as shadow minister in Opposition and had proved open to ideas about practical action to promote the growth of housing co-operatives. Wilson's decision to appoint Freeson as Minister of State for Housing in 1974 presented a golden opportunity and the Co-operative Party exploited it to the full, persuading Freeson to set up a government working party to look into ways of encouraging and assisting co-operative housing initiatives. Several of its recommendations were incorporated into the Housing Rents and Subsidies Act 1975, which, for the first time, enabled groups to form themselves into co-operatives and then, like housing associations, to seek public funding from local authorities or from the Housing Corporation. Once a scheme was built, registered rents could be passed on to the funding authority after deduction of allowances to the co-operative for management and maintenance work. Crucially, subsidies traditionally given by government to local authority housing could be transferred to other organizations, namely co-operatives.

The third great issue, the creation of a Co-operative Development Agency, proved more difficult to achieve. Despite gaining seats from the Conservatives at the October 1974 election, Wilson secured an overall majority of only three. With the Stonehouse affair and by-election defeats he was soon leading a minority government. Legislation was difficult to get through and the government focused on what Employment Secretary Michael Foot called the 'economic typhoon' blowing against them. When in the spring of 1976 Wilson unexpectedly announced his resignation as Labour leader and Prime Minister, the CDA remained a substantial piece of unfinished business.

Despite the responsibility he bore for introducing the hated Selective Employment Tax, the Co-operative Party had high hopes of James Callaghan, who succeeded Wilson as prime minister after a short leadership campaign amongst Labour MPs. Callaghan had worked closely with Co-operative MPs in the past and retained an enduring respect for Alf Barnes, whose deputy he had been at the Ministry of Transport.[105] Callaghan gave a senior role to Dickson

---

105   Callaghan's first ministerial post had been as Barnes' deputy at the Ministry of
        Transport 1947-51 and he had even tried to modify his speaking style to mimic Barnes'
        somewhat dull Commons speaking style. 'His patience and quiet approach disarmed
        the most prickly Conservative and he got his bills through the house more easily than
        other more entertaining but controversial ministers,' Callaghan recalled in his memoir.
        Barnes had also been receptive to Callaghan's successful efforts to introduce zebra
        crossings and cats eyes on the roads (civil servants claimed the latter would lead to
        more accidents from drivers converging on the centre of the road).

106   Mabon had been a key campaigner for Roy Jenkins but agreed to join Callaghan's
        campaign team when Jenkins dropped out after coming third on the first ballot.

Mabon[106] as Minister of State for Energy and deputy to Tony Benn. Mabon was also appointed to the Privy Council.[107] Of other Co-operative parliamentarians, Ted Graham and Bert Oram (to whom Wilson had given a peerage in January) were appointed to the Commons and Lords whips offices respectively. Lord Jacques (a whip under Wilson) and Alf Morris (junior minister for the disabled) continued in their posts. Callaghan also appointed James Wellbeloved, one of the three MPs sponsored by the Royal Arsenal Co-operative Society (RACS), to be Under-Secretary of State for the RAF.[108]

As the Callaghan Government got into its stride there was, initially, no sign of the promised CDA and concerns were raised at the Co-operative Party annual conference that spring. An Early Day Motion in Parliament attracted the signatures of seventy-seven MPs and a delegation of Co-operative MPs met Deputy Leader Michael Foot, Chief Whip Michael Cocks and Industry Minister Alan Williams. While the Co-operative Party awaited the CDA with baited breath, other issues raised at its conferences reflected its continuing role as a voice for the consumer. Some demands were farsighted. They included a call for government to 'compel firms to collect and recycle materials such as glass, plastics and metal'; a call to 'illegalise wasteful packaging which uses paper products, plastics and/or glass'; and a call to 'minimise the polluting effects of burning' coal, oil and gas. Others were more immediate: at the 1978 conference delegates demanded better water provision at public amenities, after a Westcountry teacher and Co-operative Party activist told delegates how the paucity of facilities at his school had prevented children from getting a drink of water amid temperatures of 114 Fahrenheit the previous summer.

On 22nd October 1977 Callaghan was guest of honour at the Co-operative Party Diamond Anniversary rally at Westminster Central Hall, celebrating the sixtieth anniversary of the Co-operative Party. There, he announced to applause that his government would ensure that a bill to establish a Co-operative Development Agency would be put through in the forthcoming parliamentary session. He was as good as his word. The CDA Bill became law on 30th June 1978, and the CDA itself was established on 1st September 1978. Lord Oram was appointed its first chairman.

---

107   From which John Stonehouse was in the process of being removed. Mabon was first Co-operative politician appointed to the Privy Council since Stonehouse, Lord Beswick and George Darling in the 1960s and they themselves were the first appointments since Alf Barnes in 1945 and AV Alexander in 1929.

108   The RACS remained unique amongst the co-operative societies in affiliating directly to the Labour Party.

DEFEAT AND DIVISION

Barely had Lord Oram got his feet under the desk at the new CDA than the Winter of Discontent torpedoed the credibility of the Callaghan government. The failure of sufficient Scottish and Welsh voters to back the 'Yes' campaign in the devolution referenda of March 1979 led to a government defeat in a vote of confidence in the House of Commons and a General Election. The personal popularity of Callaghan was to no avail. Labour trailed the Conservatives in the polls and Margaret Thatcher entered Downing Street on 3rd May 1979.

Despite an overall reduction in Labour MPs, the election saw seventeen of twenty-five Co-operative Party candidates secure seats. This was a larger number than in either of the two elections in 1974, and the Co-operative Party remained the third largest party in parliament, with five more MPs than the Liberal Party. There were two new young Co-operative MPs, both in their late thirties, co-operators to the core and future stars of the parliamentary group: George Foulkes at Ayr and Barry Sheerman at Huddersfield. Foulkes was, like Dickson Mabon, pro-devolution, and pro-EEC, but while Mabon had been at Glasgow University, Foulkes was an Edinburgh man.[109] Sheerman grew up in south-west London and after LSE spent fifteen years as a lecturer at Swansea University, where he was an enthusiastic promoter of grass-roots co-operation and had founded Wales's first 'local CDA' – in West Glamorgan. He was an energetic social-entrepreneur. Other additions to the parliamentary group since 1974 were Dick Douglas at Dunfermline[110] and former Wandsworth councillor John Tilley who had defeated the future Conservative Party chairman Jeremy Hanley to hold the Labour seat of Lambeth Central at a by-election in 1978. Numerically they more than made up for the defeat of the ageing Sydney Irving at Dartford, the retirement of Joyce Butler at Wood Green and the loss of Stonehouse's seat in 1976.

---

109   Foulkes was sufficiently passionate a Hearts football supporter that in later years he would encourage one of its star players to become Edinburgh University's first non-graduate rector. Subsequently he also became chairman of the club. At university not only had Foulkes been president of both the students' representative council and of the Scottish Union of Students, he had joined St Cuthbert's Co-operative Society. During the 1970s he had been both an Edinburgh councillor and had chaired Lothian Region Education Committee 1974-79.

110   Douglas was a former university lecturer who had served as the Co-operative MP for Clackmannan and East Stirlingshire 1970-74.

The most senior ex-minister of the group, Dickson Mabon, very nearly became the first Co-operative MP to win election to the Labour Shadow Cabinet since AV Alexander pulled it off in five successive years in 1935-39 (in 1939 Alexander had actually topped the poll).[111] Now fifty-four, Mabon's failure to secure election to the Shadow Cabinet marked the end of his front-bench career.[112] Nevertheless, the profile of the group was maintained with the appointment of two talented younger MPs to Callaghan's front-bench team: John Roper as a junior defence spokesman, and Ian Wrigglesworth as junior spokesman on the Civil Service[113] Ted Graham and Alf Morris continued to shadow the posts they had previously held in government.[114] Further additions to Co-operative strength came with the election of two out of the four Co-operative Party candidates at the UK's first direct elections to the European Parliament on 7 June 1979. These were Yorkshire councillor Brian Key and RACS political secretary Richard Balfe.

Despite the Co-operative Party's parliamentary strength, it found itself on the political defensive almost immediately. One of Margaret Thatcher's first acts was to abolish the Department of Prices and Consumer Protection, for which the Co-operative Party had lobbied so hard. Consumer affairs were relegated to a junior minister within the newly-merged Department of Trade and Industry (DTI). If there was to be a battle between business interests and the consumer, Thatcher's instincts were to support her allies in business.

The fortunes of co-operative housing, whose future following the Reg Freeson legislation in 1975 had seemed brighter, were stymied by Mrs Thatcher's determination to sell off council housing. In her critique of municipal housing management she was pushing at an open door amongst many tenants: the idea had first been suggested during the 1970 election campaign by Labour housing minister Bob Mellish and dismissed by his Tory opposite number Sir Keith

---

111   Alexander had also been Shadow Leader of the Lords 1955-64, but the Lords leader
       post was elected separately from the main Shadow Cabinet group of MPs. Since 1923,
       whenever Labour had been in opposition a 'Shadow Cabinet' has been elected by an
       annual secret ballot of MPs. To this team the leader had discretion to add extra
       spokespeople, but the elected members were supposed to be appointed to Cabinet
       should Labour form a government. Apart from 1931-35 when it was seven, the elected
       Shadow Cabinet was twelve-strong 1923-81. It was expanded to fifteen in 1981 and to
       eighteen in 1989.

112   Dickson Mabon, Interview with the author. As a backbencher, Mabon returned to pro-
       EEC campaigning as deputy chair of the cross-party European Movement.

113   There was then a Department for the Civil Service. It was abolished during the 1980s.

114   Graham had been a Lord Commissioner to the Treasury (senior whip) and Morris the
       Under-Secretary of State for Health and Social Services with responsibility for the
       disabled.

Joseph. Callaghan himself had considered introducing a right-to-buy, but had feared alienating Labour councillors. The failure of Labour councils to grasp the opportunity afforded by co-operative housing to operate public housing in a way that gave influence to tenants was one of the great lost opportunities of the era. Some had started; Richard Tomlinson, for example, remembers promoting a co-operative housing scheme in Ealing, but the Conservatives gained control of the council and ditched the scheme. One of the most successful was in the Vauxhall area of Liverpool, where the 'Eldonian' Co-operative rejuvenated and ran several hundred homes until the Militant-dominated council municipalised them in 1983.[115] The failure of councils to give tenants an effective voice in the running of municipal housing left them vulnerable to tenants seizing control of their destiny by simply buying their home off the council as Mrs Thatcher now encouraged them to do.

Most damaging though, was that in the public mind, the image of the co-operative movement had been tarnished by failure. Ironically, this was nothing to do with the ongoing battle on the high-street between the co-ops and the 'multiples'. It was the consequence of Tony Benn's adoption of ostensibly 'co-operative' solutions to some of the high-profile business collapses that occurred during his tenure as Secretary of State for Industry (1974-75). Benn's skill as a communicator meant that the co-operatives he backed were transformed into the most prominent co-operative enterprises in the country. As a result, George Foulkes believes, however well intentioned Benn's appropriation of co-operation was, he 'set the idea of worker co-operatives back a generation'. The trouble was, as Labour's then Deputy Leader Roy Hattersley lamented in his book *Choose Freedom*, that 'the status of worker co-operatives was desperately damaged by the behaviour of the [1974-79] Labour government' which used them as 'a system of outdoor relief' and 'a way of propping up firms which could not survive as independent private companies'.

They included the *Scottish Daily News*, based on the remaining plant of the *Scottish Daily Express* and KME at Kirby which manufactured car radiators and orange juice. For Roy Hattersley, 'co-operative organisation is not and cannot be an economic retreat from the realities of the market and hope for industrial incurables...[yet].. in all the discussions of Kirby's future which I attended, the prospect of its ever becoming a commercial success was never considered.'[116]

The most famous of Benn's projects was the Norton Villiers Triumph motorcycle plant at Meriden, which produced what were effectively 1950s-

---

115   Undaunted, the 'Eldonians' took over a derelict Tate and Lyle sugar factory and after
       Militant lost control over the council they were able to open one of the largest new-
       build housing co-operatives in Europe.

116   Lord Foulkes, interview with the author; Roy Hattersley, *Choose Freedom*, (London,
       1987), p 199.

technology motorcycles. They had character, but they vibrated and leaked oil. Japanese rivals were cheaper to buy, cheaper to run, often easier to handle, simpler to maintain and more reliable. In consequence, consumers were buying them instead of British motorcycles and that was why Norton Villiers Triumph was in financial difficulties. Denis Healey claimed that TGWU chief Jack Jones had told him that 'you didn't need research and development for motorcycles'.[117] Whilst it was not necessary to produce motorbikes to existing designs, it was naive to think that in a competitive world market where overseas firms were producing better designs you could do without research. The alternative was import controls, and the Soviet bloc model that meant East Berliners could choose to drive any car they liked just so long as it was a Wartburg or a Trabant. Norton Villiers Triumph motorcycles were not quite so backward and many are prized by devoted enthusiasts, but the principle was the same. Benn's scheme would ultimately fail, despite the best efforts of the workforce and supporters who included Labour MP Geoffrey Robinson, who worked as Meriden's volunteer Chief Executive 1978-80.

For the then Co-operative MP Jim Craigen, Benn's approach to co-operation was inherently flawed. He recalls: 'You have to be sensible about the economics. The workers were desperate. But if they are not viable, it gives the whole co-op ethos a bad name. The thing about the Rochdale pioneers is they kept the thing going. You have to be hard-headed. As my aunt used to say to me, "If you look after pennies the pounds will look after themselves".' [118]

Not all Co-operative Party activists agreed, despite the fact that to make uneconomic worker co-operatives viable would have required the imposition of substantial restrictions on consumer choice. The irony of belonging to a party that sought to be the voice of consumers seeking to force consumers against their will to buy poorer quality goods at inflated prices seemed entirely lost on them. Some explicitly wished the Co-operative Party to become a producer-dominated party, advocating the interests of worker-co-operatives within a socialist state that acted to minimise the impact of the market.

They demanded import controls and withdrawal from the EEC. Some of them also advocated, like Benn, closer ties with the Soviet bloc. Many felt that the co-operative movement should embrace Meriden and the other Benn-promoted worker co-operatives with greater enthusiasm. The noisiest proponents of this approach came from the London Co-operative Society (LCS), whose president, the left-wing MP Stan Newens, had published pamphlets including *The Case Against NATO and Talking with Nicolae Ceausescu – An interview with Stan*

117   Phillip Whitehead, *The Writing on the Wall*, (Michael Joseph, 1985) p 142

118   Jim Craigen, interview with the author.

Newens.[119] Until the late 1950s the LCS had been a commercially successful society run by protégés of Alf Barnes. Its political committee had been better resourced than the Co-operative Party itself – a source of some jealousy. By 1979 the LCS was in very poor shape financially, having been run into the ground by a management board controlled since the early 1960s by an electoral machine known as the 1960 Committee.[120] This was alliance of communists and employees who included the business manager of the *Daily Worker* newspaper, the secretary of the Morning Star Co-operative Society and the author of a pamphlet *Class War in the High Street*. Rather than modernise and evolve with the changing London market as the Gaitskell commission had recommended, the board allowed it to ossify, maintaining jobs and the level of dividend (despite falling surplus) by selling assets such as the Oxford Street store and putting the money into the current account.

The attraction of the LCS and other co-operative societies to the communists was that it gave them influence on the Co-operative Party and through it a Labour Government. Though Communist Party members had been formally banned from both Labour and Co-operative Party membership decades before, the structure of the Co-operative Party meant that it had representatives on its senior committees from the trading arm.[121] This meant that it was possible for communists to get elected to co-operative political committees without actually being members of the Co-operative Party: they could join a retail society and secure election as its representative onto Co-operative Party committees.

It became virtually impossible to get elected onto committees within the LCS without the imprimatur of the 1960 Committee. Andy Love, who served on the political committee during the 1980s, recalls: 'Eventually the only route into the society was through the 1960 Committee. If you stood as an independent

---

119   Stan Newens, interview with the author. Newens was Labour MP for Epping 1964-70
       and Co-operative MP for Harlow 1974-83. He was a director (1971-77) and then
       president of the London Co-operative Society (1977-81). Alf Lomas, political secretary
       of the London Co-operative Society 1965-79, proposed a resolution calling for import
       controls at the Co-operative Party conference 1977. He had published a pamphlet
       entitled *The Common Market why We Should Keep Out* in 1970.

120   The Communists tried the same tactic to take over the Royal Arsenal Co-operative
       Society but though the hard-left became a significant minority voice, the system of
       proportional representation used in internal elections prevented them ever from
       gaining sufficient representation on the board to gain control.

121   It also meant that key personnel in the trading arm might be supporters of any other
       political party. Indeed for much of the 1960s the president of Leeds Co-operative
       society was a leading Conservative. For many years many senior figures in the
       Northern Ireland co-operative movement supported the Ulster Unionists.

candidate you simply weren't going to get elected. It meant a failure to tackle vested interests and close uneconomic stores. The dominance of employees became too great and generated inefficiencies.' LCS became an early supporter of the Campaign for Nuclear Disarmament. Stan Newens contends that, 'the success of CND owed a great deal to the resources and support that the LCS Political Committee used to give it.'[122]

The LCS Political Committee became a powerhouse for the left within both the Co-operative Party and the wider Labour movement, using its ample resources to help tip the balance in London Labour politics away from the traditional approach of Herbert Morrison and Alf Barnes to the brave new world of 'Red Ted' Knight.[123] By May 1965, such was the growing influence of the hard-left on the LCS political committee that *Co-operative News* felt it necessary to attack, 'an increasingly blatant anti-Americanism; a frame of mind which puts the worst possible construction on American policy and the best possible construction on the policy of any anti-American elements wherever they are to be found...'[124]

Within the LCS sphere of influence the power of the hard-left grew. London Co-operative Parties became important bases from which to get left-wingers nominated to Labour Party management committees and to push model resolutions through Constituency Labour Parties.[125] It was a sign of the way the wind was blowing that when Joyce Butler retired as Co-operative MP for Wood Green, her successor at the 1979 election was not another co-operator but Reg Race, the hard-left NUPE organiser who had played a major behind-the-scenes role in fomenting the 'Winter of Discontent'.

As the hard-left gained ground and confidence within the Labour Party so its confidence and ambition grew. David Wise, then Co-operative Party National Secretary, remembers taking a call from miners' leader Arthur Scargill, a longstanding communist with no discernable prior interest in the Co-operative Party, requesting three hundred membership forms.[126] Wise recalls similar

---

122 Andy Love and Stan Newens, interviews with the author.

123 Ted Knight was the leader of Lambeth council from 1978 until he was banned from elected office in 1986 as a result of being surcharged for his refusal to set a legal rate. He had originally been expelled from the Labour Party in 1956 for his involvement with the Socialist Labour League – Trotskyist forerunner of the Workers' Revolutionary Party for whom he worked until 1961. He had been readmitted to the Labour Party in 1970.

124 *Co-operative Party Monthly Letter*, May 1965, pp 10-12

125 They affiliated on basis of numbers in area with a divvy, not party members, so always got maximum numbers of delegates (five to each local Labour Party constituency general committee).

126 David Wise, interview with the author.

attempts at mass infiltration in Liverpool and east London. Eventually Wise and other moderates were able to reform the party rulebook so that before someone could be a delegate to another body such as a Constituency Labour Party management committee, they were required to have been a Co-operative Party member for a minimum of two years, and to be a member of a co-operative organisation[127] thus frustrating the so-called 'bed-sit Trotskyites' who sought to move between constituencies to influence the reselection of MPs.

The Co-operative Party found itself dragged reluctantly into the battle that raged for the soul of the Labour Party between the adherents of Tony Benn and the moderates. The Co-operative Party 1979 annual report set out a clear policy vision that to the Bennites must have resembled a red rag to a bull:

'We have regarded it as a principal function of the Party to demand the organisation and government of society so that the maximum degree of free and voluntary association is provided. Our Labour Party allies have not always followed this precept. This is largely because the emphasis of Labour Party thinking has been the interest of the producer in the form of the organised worker. For many years we have questioned the validity of nationalisation as the ultimate development of socialism and claim that it does not in fact mean consumer control, since it encourages uniformity rather than diversity.... Co-operators are by natural inclination social democrats. They believe that power belongs to the people, authority rests on consent and should be granted, sparingly, to those leaders chosen by the community. And those leaders should at all times be accountable... we advocate co-operation as the form of social ownership most likely to succeed. It will succeed because it attracts the support of those engaged in the enterprise. The Co-operative form of social ownership is the alternative to nationalisation and state ownership. Nationalisation is right for some industries but not for all... The state is not always the same thing as the community...'

Benn's supporters were determined to ensure that a future Labour government consigned such ideas to the dustbin of political history. If the Co-operative Party was a consumer party mitigating Labour's bias towards producer-dominated politics, then the Bennites were suspicious for that very reason. Moreover, Alun Michael believes, 'Labour's public sector people feared the Co-operative Party was a Trojan horse to break up the monolithic public sector.'[128]

---

127   For example a shop or to have an account with the bank.
128   Co-operative Party 1979 annual conference annual report, p 24; Alun Michael, interview with the author.

At the Labour Party annual conference in September 1979, the main debate on future policy was a battle between a moderate resolution moved by Co-operative Party MP Mike Thomas and a left-wing counter-resolution demanding 'the nationalisation of the top two hundred or so monopolies'. For Thomas, the consequences of the hard-left agenda were all too visible in the London Co-operative Society which, after nearly twenty years of management by the communists and their allies on the 1960 Committee, was facing financial collapse. It was saved only by the transfer of its engagements to the Co-operative Retail Society in January 1981. The CRS swiftly announced a programme of significant redundancies at the LCS Stratford back-office. At the 1980 Labour conference Tony Benn declared that he shared the 'deep socialist conviction' of the Militant activists who moved a resolution demanding that redundancies be banned and that any business threatening redundancies be nationalised.

This was not the first time the Labour Party had swung to the left. On previous occasions the moderates had regrouped and brought Labour's helm back to a more social-democratic course. When Gaitskell was defeated over unilateral nuclear disarmament in 1960, he famously pledged to 'fight and fight and fight again to save the party I love' and successfully reversed the conference vote the following year, bringing Labour policy back to supporting a multilateral approach. This time was different. Having seen previous victories rolled back, the hard-left hoped that securing three key changes to the Labour Party constitution would enable them to ratchet policy irreversibly to the left. Many moderate MPs began to fear that Labour's commitments to unilateral nuclear disarmament, to withdrawal from the EEC without a referendum and for a substantial programme of nationalisation would be irreversible.

During 1979-81 the hard-left bulldozed through these three changes to the Labour Party constitution, transferring power from the MPs and Labour Party leadership, whom they considered insufficiently radical, to constituency party activists and trade union barons. First they changed the leadership election process, from a ballot amongst MPs to an electoral college where union block votes would carry the day.[129] Second, MPs were to be required to undergo 'mandatory reselection' to turn them from representatives of their voters into delegates of local Labour activists. Thirdly the Labour leader and Shadow Cabinet lost their veto over items for inclusion in the manifesto, which would from now on be controlled exclusively by Labour's National Executive Committee.

---

129   They rejected one-member-one-vote, claiming in the words of Michael Meacher, then
         a leading Benn supporter, that it would give too much power to the 'media.'

It was against that background that the 'Gang of Four' former cabinet ministers (Roy Jenkins, David Owen, Bill Rodgers and Shirley Williams) broke away from Labour to form the Social Democratic Party (SDP) in March 1981. Among the dozen MPs who joined them at the launch were three of the Co-operative Party's most prominent younger MPs - John Roper, Mike Thomas and Ian Wrigglesworth. As 1981 wore on the rows intensified. Labour leader Michael Foot has described the misery of the era: 1981 'could have been the [year] in which the Labour movement applied all its energies to concert united vengeance for the wounds inflicted upon our people and to destroy the Tory government. Instead we turned it into a period of futility and shame and the responsibility for transmuting every controversy of the time into an internal Labour Party dispute rested directly with Tony Benn.'[130] The autumn of 1981 was taken up by Tony Benn's attempt to unseat Denis Healey as Labour's deputy leader. Healey held on by a tight margin (50.43% to 49.57%) but one of those for whom the feuding proved too much was Dickson Mabon, who joined the SDP that October. Thus the Co-operative Party lost four of seventeen MPs, including two of its shadow ministers and one of its only Privy Counsellors in the Commons.[131] It was a blow both to its credibility and cohesion. A further loss to the SDP was the Co-operative peer Lord Taylor of Gryfe, a former president of the Scottish Co-operative Wholesale Society. Additionally both John Cartwright and James Wellbeloved – two of the three south-east London RACS-sponsored MPs – defected to the SDP during 1981.[132]

Some journalists took at face value SDP claims that the Co-operative Party as a whole was going to break off its alliance with Labour and forge a new one with the SDP. As a result the 1981 Co-operative Party conference was unusually well-furnished with TV cameras. But the journalists were largely disappointed. Few Co-operative Party activists followed the lead of the defecting MPs and specific attempts by the SDP to recruit further defectors amongst parliamentarians – such as Lord Oram – proved unsuccessful. Nevertheless, as David Wise recalls, it became a real battle for survival.[133]

During what was a chaotic and turbulent political time, there was a significant risk that the confidence of the retail societies in the future of the Party might disintegrate. Without the confidence and finance of the co-operative movement the Party could not exist. The chaos caused by the SDP split and the

---

130   Michael Foot, *Loyalists and Loners*, (Collins, 1986), p 122

131   The other was Alf Morris who had been appointed in 1979.

132   The remaining RACS-sponsored MP, Harry Lamborn at Peckham, died the following year.

133   Interviews with the author (Lady Oram, Ted Graham, George Foulkes, Dickson Mabon, David Wise and others).

plunging popularity of the Labour Party, to which the Co-operative Party remained allied, provided, as Andy Love recalls,[134] an all too convenient scapegoat for co-operative managers wanting to find something to blame for their declining sales performance. For some years there had been managers who claimed all would be well were their potential customers not put off by the association of the movement – through the Party – with 'politics'. Now they had their pretext. Adrian Bailey[135] is not alone in believing that 'sustaining the support of the retail movement for the Party at a time when the retail movement was in dire financial difficulties was a reflection of the political skill of David Wise and his team'. Wise had a credibility that straddled both the Party and the movement. Indeed by the end of the 1980s he would be criticised by some for spending too little time with the Party on account of his role as chairman of the CIS, which had him working in Manchester three days a week. In the dark days of the early 1980s, however, his role on the boards of the Invicta Co-op in Kent and of the CIS were vital assets. Bailey's colleague Richard Tomlinson recalls: 'Wise kept the finances in one piece. He kept the co-op movement and Co-operative Party going in the same direction. If the Co-operative Party had gone politically to the Left then co-operative societies would have stopped financing it.'[136]

In Wise's own mind, 'the most important thing was keeping the link with Labour'. He recalls, 'at that time it was at its nadir.'[137] The increasingly dominant Benn agenda meant, as Alun Michael remembers, that 'in politics it became not somehow respectable to be a co-operator. *Militant* and the public sector unions were both dominant in the Labour Party and emphasising the public sector. I was struck that nobody mentioned the voluntary sector at Labour meetings. It was similar if people had experience in business, the co-operative movement or were Christian socialists. Co-operative ideas were pushed out of the mainstream during the 1980s.'[138]

---

134   Andy Love MP, interview with the author.

135   Interview with the author. Bailey has been a Co-operative MP since a by-election in 2000. During the 1980s and 1990s regional organizer for the Midlands and South Yorkshire

136   Interview with Richard Tomlinson. Tomlinson was then the Southern Regional Organiser for the Co-operative Party.

137   Interview with the author

138   Alun Michael interview with the author. Michael became Co-operative MP for Cardiff South and Penarth in 1987 and served as a senior minister for most of the period 1997-2006, including a stint in Cabinet as Secretary of State for Wales. He was also first leader of the Wales Assembly Government. A former journalist on the *South Wales Echo*, during the 1980s Michael was Constituency Secretary to former Prime Minister James Callaghan.

If co-operative ideas were on the defensive vis-à-vis the Labour Party, then a series of disastrous by-election results soon showed that Labour was on the ropes vis-à-vis the electorate. The first came in 1981 after Tom Williams, veteran Co-operative MP and barrister, accepted a post as a High Court Judge. This required him to stand down from his parliamentary seat at Warrington. The by-election was the first to be contested by the new SDP and their candidate, Roy Jenkins, secured such a substantial swing in the vote that he almost won what had been a safe seat.

Subsequent by-elections saw several spectacular SDP and Liberal victories. Even where the seats had been Conservative held, as at Crosby and Glasgow Hillhead which were won by Shirley Williams and Roy Jenkins respectively for the SDP, Labour's vote was pulverised. Labour's credibility not only as an alternative government but as the main Opposition party was called seriously into question, as by-election victories helped the SDP rocket ahead in the opinion polls.

From Labour's by-election disasters sprung an opportunity for the Co-operative Party to demonstrate its continuing political salience. Two crucial pins that punctured the SDP balloon were the by-elections at Birmingham Northfield in October 1982 and at Darlington in March 1983. At Northfield, the agent was Dick Knowles, a former Co-operative Party national organiser who would subsequently become Leader of Birmingham council. His deputy was the then Co-operative Party regional organiser Adrian Bailey (subsequently an MP). The candidate, John Spellar was head of research for the EETPU electricians union but knew and valued the Co-operative Party from his own co-operative involvement in south-east London and Kent. Adrian Bailey recalls: 'The Co-operative party was crucial to winning Northfield by-election. Co-op activists in the area including Clive Wilkinson kept Birmingham and the Black Country moderate, working closely with unions like the GMB and EETPU.' The campaigning skills of the Co-operative Party organisers played a critical role in helping Spellar secure a vital victory: it was the first seat that Labour had won from the Conservatives at a by-election since 1971 and was a feat that Labour was unable to repeat until Nick Raynsford won the Fulham by-election in 1986. If Northfield had given Labour renewed heart, Darlington almost shattered Labour's patched-up credibility. The SDP selected a high-profile TV presenter as their candidate and initially looked set to win the seat off Labour. This time, the candidature was secured by the Co-operative Party for the director of studies at the Co-operative College, Ossie O'Brien. In contrast to the hard-left candidates selected by Labour at by-election disasters such as Bermondsey (1982), O'Brien's moderate approach and the active involvement in the campaign of all five Co-operative Party regional organisers, personally supervised by David Wise, turned round the campaign and elected another Co-operative MP.

A CO-OPERATIVE VIEW OF SOCIALISM

Despite the by-election success at Darlington, Labour's catastrophic performance at the 1983 general election, a bare eleven weeks later, saw the number of Co-operative MPs reduced to seven (from seventeen candidates). Perhaps the only consolation was that they were now larger than the SDP who had been reduced from some thirty MPs to a mere six. Four seats had been lost where the MPs had joined the SDP.[139] Several of the remaining Co-operative MPs, including Ted Graham, Stan Newens and Ossie O'Brien, were defeated at the election. Two further casualties were the ageing Arthur Palmer at Bristol North-East and the new MP John Tilley at Lambeth Central, both of whose seats were abolished by boundary changes. While Palmer retired, Tilley sought unsuccessfully to win Bermondsey off Liberal MP Simon Hughes. Ted Graham, who as a Shadow Environment Minister 1981-83 had been the most senior of the Co-operative MPs, was appointed to the Lords in Foot's 'resignation honours,' and was immediately back on the front-bench, but the experience of 1979-83 and the loss of so many talented MPs undoubtedly diminished the Co-operative Party's parliamentary voice.

The poor financial performance of the wider co-operative movement continued to prompt questions in some quarters about whether the party was an unaffordable luxury. For Wise and his team, fending these off was a major priority. The 1984 European elections afforded a brief respite from the gloom. All three Co-operative Party candidates were elected (Brian Key did not stand, having been deselected by an NUM-backed campaign to replace him with a candidate more politically acceptable to Arthur Scargill). The three were the former RACS political secretary Richard Balfe and former MPs Stan Newens and John Tomlinson. Though Tomlinson had previously been a Labour rather than a Co-operative Party MP (for Meriden 1974-79) he was 'family': his brother Richard was the Co-operative Party southern regional organiser and he himself was a graduate of the Co-operative College and had been secretary of Sheffield Co-operative Party 1961-68. He had also been a high flyer, having been PPS to Prime Minister Harold Wilson 1975-76 and a junior minister at the Foreign Office and Ministry of Overseas Development 1976-79. Had he not lost his seat in 1979 he would have been a senior figure on the Labour benches and he was a valued addition to Co-operative ranks in the European parliament.

---

139   Of the Co-operative and RACS MPs who joined the SDP, only Ian Wrigglesworth and John Cartwright, held their seats – though Mabon and Wellbeloved were amongst the handful of SDP MPs whose defeat was narrow.

Neil Kinnock, who replaced Michael Foot as Labour leader after the 1983 election, promoted several Co-operative MPs to his new Opposition team. Jim Craigen, who had been chair of the Employment Select Committee 1982-83 was appointed an Opposition front-bench spokesman on Scotland, George Foulkes on Europe, and Barry Sheerman on employment and education. Alf Morris continued as Shadow Minister for the Disabled. More than half the Co-operative Party MPs were now shadow ministers.[140] But it was not just the frontbenchers who were active. Laurie Pavitt made a name for himself as an anti-smoking campaigner with a series of private member's bills seeking the restriction of tobacco advertising. Outside parliament, the Co-operative Party was voicing concern on wider ethical issues. In 1986, for example, the Co-operative Party conference voted to urge local co-operative retail societies to boycott South African goods.

In the Labour Party, Neil Kinnock and his allies on the Bevanite 'soft-left' forged an alliance with Roy Hattersley and John Smith from the old Gaitskellite 'right' to roll back the influence of Militant and the Bennite hard-left. But Labour's policy approach remained essentially defensive and statist. It was about denouncing the consequences of Thatcherism, and pulling back from the hard-left policy pledges that had made Labour unelectable in 1983 and 1987. Even in 1987 Labour's private polling showed that 78% of voters still thought Labour 'extremist' and at no stage during 1982-87 had more than one quarter of the electorate felt that Labour's defence policies came closest to their own. The British Social Attitudes survey showed that nationalisation had not been supported by more than one third of the electorate since 1964 and that 56% of the electorate believed that an economic crisis was more likely under Labour.[141]

As early as 1985, the Co-operative Party had begun the quiet process of reasserting itself as the legitimate voice of consumers in politics. At the Co-operative Party conference in the spring of 1985, six months before Neil Kinnock's famous 'I'm telling you and you'll listen' speech denouncing *Militant* at the 1985 Labour Party conference, the Co-operative Party published *The Co-operative View of Socialism*. Drafted by National Secretary David Wise it was published with the full endorsement of the Party National Executive. In deference to the political realities governing the state of debate within the Labour Party at that time, it conceded that coal, steel, gas, electricity, water, rail and the post office should 'remain in public ownership'. Nevertheless it was quietly damning of the statism then dominating Labour thinking:

---

140   Ioan Evans, backbench Co-operative MP for Cynon Valley, died less than a year after the 1983 election.

141   Colin Hughes and Patrick Wintour, *Labour Rebuilt*, (Fourth Estate, 1990) p 62

'Many perceive socialism and public ownership as being synonymous with nationalisation and the remote bureaucratic state monopoly which is owned by the state, directed by state appointees and is operated in a way which satisfies neither consumers nor workers, and which appears to be of little or no practical benefit to the general public... sadly, public experience has generated hostility to rather than enthusiasm for the existing nationalised undertakings.'

Instead it sought to harness the empowering role of decentralisation in a way that Labour had yet to explore:

'We favour rapid and decisive moves towards decentralisation of government services and administration. The centripetal forces of the Whitehall machine have, we maintain, meant that the Executive, Parliament and the state bureaucracy have become increasingly overburdened and often totally out of touch with what is needed in the localities. Ministers and civil servants become increasingly unaccountable and administration is often effected on the basis of rigidly applied rules operated without regard to humanity or the real needs of those at the receiving end. The clash between those who favour the concentration of all decision making at the centre and those who wish to encourage choice, diversity, experiment, local initiative and enterprise, has been at the forefront of political debate for some time, but the autocratic and even dictatorial policies of the Conservative government has added a new dimension to this debate.'

Not until Tony Blair would a Labour leader grasp the 'choice and diversity' agenda raised by the Co-operative Party in 1985, and not until Gordon Brown, the first Prime Minister to be a Co-operative Party member, would there be a Prime Minister who understood the Co-operative Party critique of centralised government.

Several heavyweight players in local government circles were members of the Co-operative Party. Amongst them were the leaders of Birmingham, Sandwell and Nottingham Councils. *The Co-operative View of Local Government*, published at the 1987 Co-operative Party conference, took the theme of *The Co-operative View of Socialism* and applied it to the challenge of rejuvenating local councils. It anticipated the approach taken in the local government reforms post-1997:

'We are opposed to the injustice which a remote and unaccountable local bureaucracy can inflict upon communities. We also oppose inefficiency in local government because it is an undemocratic denial of other people's, groups' and communities' opportunities... Decentralisation will be a failure unless it involves local people influencing decision-making processes... there is a case for leaders and deputy leaders of councils and some committee chairs being full-time...'

An understandable reluctance to stir up more opposition to Neil Kinnock's attempts to beat back the left within the Labour Party meant that the Co-operative Party did not seek policy concessions from the Labour Party reflecting *The Co-operative View of Socialism* and *The Co-operative View of Local Government*. There was a further reason: finance. The continued decline of the co-operative movement's trading position through the early and mid-1980s, and the consequent amalgamation and closure of many societies meant that money for the Party was becoming ever tighter.

In consequence, from 1984 until 1988 the Co-operative Party was in deficit, forcing David Wise to implement economy measures. Posts at head-office were left unfilled, including the roles of assistant secretary and regional organiser for the North-West and Yorkshire. Wise recognised that the Party had to be financially secure in order to operate effectively. That meant minimising controversy and reminding the trading side of the co-operative movement of the lobbying benefit it gained from funding the Co-operative Party. This was not always easy, particularly in Opposition. Jim Craigen summed up the problem pithily: 'It is difficult for the Co-operative Party to oblige like a vending machine as some would have it by giving immediate returns.'[142]

It is this that helps explain why opposition to Sunday retail trading featured as one of the few overt pledges in the cursory document that was the 1987 Co-operative Party election manifesto, *Time for Change*, which, for diplomatic reasons, essentially echoed Labour's own manifesto.[143] The battle against Sunday trading caused Margaret Thatcher's greatest parliamentary defeat: on 14th April 1986. It was the one and only time that her government lost a bill on second reading in the Commons and only the second defeat of a government bill on second reading since 1924. It was, moreover, a substantial achievement for the Co-operative Party in parliament on behalf of the co-operative retail movement

---

142   Jim Craigen, *Co-operative News*, 12 October 1977.

143   It was distinctive mainly in its opposition to Sunday trading and its support for co-operative housing, for co-operative enterprise, for greater environmental protection, and for regional devolution to England as well as to Wales and Scotland

– for it had been Lord Graham who had marshalled the forces[144] in the Lords that fatally delayed her bill. That delay was sufficient for the 'Keep Sunday Special' campaign to subsequently persuade enough Conservative MPs (seventy-two) to defy a three-line whip to defeat the government.[145]

Despite the financial pressures, the Co-operative Party put up nineteen candidates at the 1987 general election (two more than in 1983) and increased its representation from six MPs to nine – nearly double the size of the SDP who had shrunk to five. Of the Co-operative MPs, the octogenarian Bob Edwards and the septuagenarian Laurie Pavitt both retired from parliament, as did the still-young Jim Craigen who went to run the Scottish Federation of Housing Associations. Five of the nine MPs were therefore new. In contrast to previous intakes, all five (Tommy McAvoy, John McFall, Alun Michael, Lewis Moonie and Dennis Turner) were to serve in Labour's front-bench team in government, in opposition, or in both.

In addition to the campaign against Sunday trading, the other great battle for Co-operative Party MPs during the late 1980s was over the decision by the Conservative government during 1988 to scrap the Co-operative Development agency (CDA). For Rita Rhodes, who worked as its education officer, the CDA was killed off by a combination of Conservative underfunding and the 'stranglehold' established by the hierarchical and bureaucratic civil service culture which stifled any co-operative ethos it might have had. Lady Oram recalls that 'not everyone on the CDA board was a co-operator. They were good people but didn't understand what the co-operative movement was all about.'[146]

The CDA was not a failure. In the Commons debate on its closure in January 1989, John McFall, chair of the Parliamentary Co-operative Group emphasised that, 'in 1978 when the CDA started, there were one hundred and eighty co-operatives. Ten years later, in March 1988 there were two thousand. It has been

---

144   Margaret Thatcher had made a profound tactical error by introducing what proved to be a controversial bill first in the Lords (rather than in the Commons as per convention). The Lords were more difficult for her to control. Graham used his skill as a whip to forge a wide-ranging coalition that included former Prime Minister Harold Macmillan and the High Court judge Lord Denning. The Commons then followed their lead.

145   The ongoing battle to resist the introduction of Sunday trading battle became one of the main priorities for the Co-operative Party during the late 1980s and in November 1988 the Co-operative MPs supported the launch of REST – the campaign to oppose Sunday trading. Some individual co-op societies (eg Devon CRS) advocated allowing restricted Sunday trading so long as there was full protection for employees who didn't wish to work on Sundays

146   Joan Oram. Interview with author.

estimated that twenty-five thousand jobs have been created in worker co-operatives since 1978 at an average cost of £3,500 per job.' But it was not nearly as successful as had been hoped and the prevailing view amongst Co-operative MPs was that there were better ways to achieve what the CDA had been set up to do.[147]

With the benefit of hindsight, there was a legitimate question to be asked about how effective a national office staffed by civil servants could ever be in helping co-operatives operate more effectively in a market economy. 'Failure was inherent within the structure,' believes Adrian Bailey. The era when the CDA had been originally conceived, as Andy Love put it, was 'the fag-end of big-government labourism.' For Love and Bailey, the CDA 'would have done better to operate locally.'[148] Indeed both Barry Sheerman and Alun Michael had been active in establishing successful local CDAs in Wales. In the Commons debate, Co-operative spokesmen John McFall and Alun Michael argued for government support for local CDAs. In a concession to Co-operative Party MPs, the Conservative minister announced that the new chairs of Training and Enterprise Councils would be made aware of co-operative options.

The Co-operative Party response to the closure of the CDA was not knee-jerk oppositionalism, but a reappraisal of the institution, considered as a means to an end rather than an end in itself. Crosland would have been proud. This approach was also evident in the Co-operative Party response to the Tory privatisations. Thus, in a 1990 pamphlet entitled *The Co-operative Way*, written by a team of Co-operative parliamentarians including John McFall, Alun Michael, and Lords Gallagher, Graham and Oram, the Co-operative Party broke with Labour's demand for the re-nationalisation of the water companies, instead calling for more research on how to transform privatised water companies into co-operatives.

At the same time, David Wise continued the process of protecting the party financially. He relocated the party head-office in July 1990 from Victoria to 342 Hoe Street, Walthamstow.[149] It was much criticised by some staff who resented the move out of the 'Westminster Village'. The upside, recalls Richard Tomlinson, one of the regional organisers, was the boost it gave to the financial security of

---

147   2007 figures contained in the Treasury Review of co-operative legislation (p 7) show that worker co-operatives in Great Britain had reduced in number to 373 with 2,067 employees and a turnover of some £130m. In contrast agricultural co-operatives in England and Scotland alone turn over £4.4bn and employ 7,863. Consumer co-operatives employ 111,205 and turn over £12.5bn.

148   Adrian Bailey MP and Andy Love MP. Interviews with the author.

149   The move had been precipitated by their landlord requiring them to give up prematurely their leasehold on 158 Buckingham Palace Road in Victoria (its location since moving from 54 Victoria Street in 1963).

the party: 'Wise said the Hoe Street building was our redundancy pay if anything goes wrong. He had to make sure the staff were looked after.'[150]

The move to Walthamstow doubled the party's operating surplus in 1990 and helped fund further election successes. The Co-operative Party group in the European parliament had already expanded with the election of Pauline Green, a former Woodcraft Folk[151] leader, police officer and Co-operative Union official, as MEP for London North in June 1989. At Westminster the group gained Gordon McMaster, a horticulturalist and former leader of Renfrew council, who fought off a strong SNP challenge to win the Paisley South by-election in November 1990. This helped to compensate for the defection to the SNP of Dick Douglas, MP for Dunfermline West since 1983 (and for East Stirlingshire 1970-74). Douglas had felt that the Labour Party was taking an insufficiently militant attitude to the poll tax and refused to accept Labour's opposition to the SNP-supported 'Can't pay, won't pay!' campaign.

In the 1992 General Election the Co-operative Parliamentary Group expanded to fourteen, more than half as large again as the group elected in 1987. It also marked the retirement of David Wise, who had served the party as national secretary for almost two decades. The succession was hotly contested and to the surprise of some (who expected one of several regional organisers to be appointed), the appointment went to Dr Peter Clarke, familiar to many in the party by his trademark fedora, who had been research officer since the 1970s.

The stable financial situation Wise had established gave Clarke a solid base from which to work and while Party membership was lower than it had been thirty years before, the Parliamentary Group was larger and more heavy-hitting than it had been for more than twenty years.[152] It included several MPs who had built up considerable reputations as talented shadow ministers, including George Foulkes, John McFall, Alun Michael, Lewis Moonie and Barry Sheerman. In addition, Tommy McAvoy had already cultivated a formidable reputation as an Opposition Whip in the Commons, while in the Lords Ted Graham had secured election as Opposition Chief Whip in 1990. Graham therefore became the first Co-operative parliamentarian in the Shadow Cabinet since Lord Beswick, who served in the same role 1970-74.

Another boost was the resurgence in the trading side of the co-operative movement. A vital catalyst for that change was the Co-operative Bank, whose

---

150   Richard Tomlinson, interview with the author.

151   The Woodcraft Folk were founded in 1925 by the co-operative movement as an equivalent organisation to the Scouts. It is a democratic organisation and its ethos contrasts with the militarist roots of the Scouts. Its motto is *Span the world with friendship.*

152   Membership was estimated at some 10,000 as compared to about 15-20,000 in the 1960s – there was not yet a national membership system.

turnaround helped improve the image and performance across the movement as a whole. Adrian Bailey remembers:

'When I joined the Co-operative Party in 1982 the Co-op Bank was synonymous with inefficiency and inflexibility. A decade later it was turning around. Labour branches had accounts with it. Terry Thomas transformed it with a business plan and ethical trading.' In addition, the Co-operative Bank secured substantial amounts from local authority accounts.

Thomas, created Lord Thomas of Macclesfield in 1997 in recognition of his achievements, saw his approach not as soulless modernisation but as a return to the roots of the co-operative movement. He recalls:

'The person who inspired me was Robert Owen. I researched the founding of the bank in 1872. I went back to the history and asked: "What were the values that inspired the bank when it was formed?"When I introduced the concept of ethics into banking most bankers thought I was crazy. One asked if I was mispronouncing "Essex"! But suddenly bank deposits increased. Much to my surprise the corporate sector was just as enthusiastic. Charles Darwin talked not of the survival of the fittest but of the most adaptable – the Tories misunderstood that.' For George Foulkes, it was 'significant that the bank got enthusiastic about fair trade and ethical investment.That enthused a lot of younger people who had never thought about the co-op.'[153]

The Co-operative Bank was soon doing so well that the Liberal Democrats set up a special visa account with it for LibDem members, much to the chagrin of Wessex CRS co-operative Party who strongly denounced it at the 1991 Co-operative Party conference. Fortunately for ruffled feathers, the Labour Party had already done the same.

Thomas was not just an idealist; he was also a good businessman. Over the next decade the co-operative movement was to transform itself financially, the process accelerating with the appointment of Sir Graham Melmoth as chief executive of the Co-operative Wholesale Society in 1996. Following the merger of the CWS with the Co-operative Retail Society in 2000, Melmoth would become chief executive of the Co-operative Group. Changes came swiftly. In 1998, the CWS reintroduced the 'divvy' as a method of returning profits and benefits to members. Given that it was at the heart of the original co-operative movement – and was what differentiated them from privately owned supermarkets – it struck many as bizarre that it had been allowed to lapse in the first place.[153*] But

---

153   Adrian Bailey and Lord Thomas, interviews with author.

153*   As profit margins were squeezed during the 1970s, many co-ops allowed the divvy to lapse, forgetting the importance of a divvy to attracting customers.

that was the situation Melmoth inherited. By 2002, the dividend program was in place throughout the Cooperative Group, with the new dividend card providing a somewhat greater return to members than the loyalty cards of rival supermarket chains. Indeed the supermarket loyalty cards were if anything a recognition of the importance of the 'divvy', if only a pale pastiche.

An *Observer* profile in 2002 judged:

'In Melmoth's six years at the helm, the co-op, based in Manchester, has almost shed its image as a regional basket-case in need of professional management. It would be fair to say that some of his achievements have astonished the City... Its supermarkets, with their stress on health and value for money, could be on course to become, in the words of one analyst, 'the Body Shop of food retailing'. And last year the Co-op Bank reported £100 million in pre-tax profits, a 10% rise.'[154]

In 2004, the Cooperative Group increased its share of the food retail market from 5% to 6% – the first increase for decades. In recognition of its pioneering work with fair trade wine, that same year it won the 'Retailer of the Year – Innovation' award at the wine world's largest competition, the International Wine Challenge.

---

154 *Observer*, 27 January 2002

A NEW MUTUALISM

The 1997 election result – twenty-eight Co-operative Party MPs – was a record. The previous highest total, in 1945, had been twenty-three. The result reflected not only the pro-Labour and anti-Tory swing achieved by Tony Blair, but also the high priority that party secretary Peter Clarke had given to encouraging Co-operative Parties at local level to be more pro-active in their involvement with parliamentary candidate selection. Since the 1958 Labour/Co-operative agreement which had imposed a maximum cap on Co-operative Party parliamentary candidates at thirty, this had been a difficult figure on which to improve. One of Peter Clarke's most significant and symbolic achievements was the new agreement negotiated with Labour in 1996 which formally removed the cap.

Tony Blair appointed several Co-operative MPs to his government. They included Alun Michael as Minister of State at the Home Office, George Foulkes as Under-Secretary of State at the new Department for International Development and Tommy McAvoy, John Owen Jones and John McFall as senior whips.[155] The great surprise concerned the post of Lords Chief Whip. Ted Graham had been highly effective as Opposition Chief Whip under first Kinnock, then Smith and now Blair in co-ordinating opposition forces in the Lords, exploiting Tory rebellions and harrying the Major government in the one place where it could lose votes. Whipping the Lords was a particular skill – many peers were fiercely independent-minded. Assembling this disparate band into an anti-Tory team required skill, patience and an ability to work with an extraordinary range of people. On the eve of the election, the Labour leader in the Lords, Lord Richard, wrote a note to Tony Blair recommending that in the event of a Labour victory Ted Graham be appointed Government Chief Whip: 'Ted Graham is the obvious and best candidate for the job... Frankly, I think he is the only person who can be guaranteed to produce the attendance necessary from our somewhat elderly troops to make sure that we can keep a House.'[156] In the event Blair preferred a younger man. He may well have suffered more rebellions in consequence. Graham became chair of the UK Co-operative

---

155   Tommy McAvoy was appointed pairing whip, the third most senior position in the whips office. Such was his effectiveness that he would ultimately become the longest-serving pairing whip since records began.

156   Cited in Janet Jones, *Labour of Love*, (Politicos, 1999)

Council, chair of the Labour Peers Group, and a sprightly septuagenarian backbencher.

Though his new Labour Party Clause IV reads as if it had been written by a co-operator, Tony Blair had no particular history in the co-operative movement, unlike James Callaghan, who had grown up shopping with it, and John Smith, who had been President of the Industrial Co-operative Movement. Blair's main connection was through Alun Michael, his deputy when Blair had been shadow Home Secretary under John Smith. Michael was one of those who sent Blair suggestions for rewriting Clause IV. They had forged a strong working relationship and Michael had made a point of introducing Blair to Co-operative Party members.

Despite the bridge that existed in the form of Alun Michael, whom Blair appointed Secretary of State for Wales in 1998 (making him the first Co-operative Party Cabinet minister since AV Alexander in 1951), Peter Clarke failed to forge as strong a relationship with Blair's Downing Street as David Wise had managed with the Callaghan premiership. Clarke concentrated his energies on persuading Blair to commit to introducing a catch-all Co-operative Act to boost the status of co-operatives within the economy. To help the process along, the co-operative movement had undertaken a great deal of preparatory work and had already produced a draft bill containing some one hundred and thirty clauses.

Nevertheless, the obstacles to progressing the draft Co-operative Bill proved of greater substance and complexity than Clarke probably realised. For a start it would have amended the Industrial and Provident Societies legislation that affects some nine thousand organisations in the UK ranging from allotment societies via British Legion clubs and the Womens' Institute markets, to Conservative Clubs. But there had not been wider consultation involving the organisations outside the co-operative movement who would have been affected. This process would have been substantial and might not have secured unanimous endorsement.

Adrian Bailey, then the Midlands and South Yorkshire party organiser, recalls: 'Even the co-operative movement was ambiguous about it. It would have taken up the first eighteen months to two years of a Labour government. The Co-operatives Bill was trumpeted as an all-embracing panacea but was a non-starter.' Ted Graham, who did what he could to persuade the government to consider taking a Co-operatives Bill forward remembers: 'There was a period when the co-operative movement expected more than Labour could deliver.'[157]

The Co-operative Act became the totemic issue for Clarke's time as national secretary and the party became bogged down in its inability to persuade the government to commit the considerable amount of parliamentary time that would have been necessary to get it through. With Clarke committing much of the rest of his time to a complex attempt to revise the Party rules relating to

---

157   Adrian Bailey and Lord Graham, interviews with the author.

expulsions, frustration grew that the party was failing to engage effectively with the new Labour Government.

In the late summer of 1997 Clarke resigned. The former Co-operative Party MP John Tilley, then secretary of the parliamentary office at the Co-operative Union, became de-facto acting Party Secretary until March 1998, when the formal process of choosing Clarke's successor was completed. The new General Secretary (as the role became) was the energetic Co-operative Party southern regional organiser Peter Hunt. At thirty-one, Hunt was considerably younger than Clarke. A former social housing manager, he had worked for the Co-operative Party since 1994.

Hunt's immediate priority was to formally secure the position of the Party. There had been renewed rumblings in Peter Clarke's time from some quarters of the Labour Party who would have liked direct access to the Co-operative Party's resources and resented its existence as a separate party. A Co-operative Party Commission, chaired by Lord Davies of Coity, the former general secretary of USDAW,[157*] reiterated the position of the Co-operative Party as the political voice of the co-operative movement and ended the direct affiliation to Labour of the continuing political committees of the old London societies (LCS and RACS). It also agreed to give individual party members their own representatives on the party national executive for the first time, to open up membership beyond consumer co-ops to other mutuals and to update the clause in the Co-operative Party constitution relating to aims and values: the Co-operative Party's 'Clause IV'. The new clause was passed unanimously at the 1999 Party Conference. The Monks Commission, chaired by TUC general secretary John Monks, which like the Gaitskell Commission of 1957-58 looked at the co-operative movement rather than the Party, also recommended that that co-op political involvement should be through the Co-operative Party.

Hunt's other priority was to rejuvenate the credibility of party policy. For Hunt this was about 'ensuring there is a firm evidence base for anything we call for and a means to deliver.' He re-launched the members' magazine as *New Mutualism* and began a series of new 'freethinking' pamphlets under the same banner. They included a pamphlet on co-operation and social exclusion by Ian Hargreaves, one on the still relatively new phenomena of the internet ('*e-mutualism*'), and *New Mutualism – a new solution for renewed councils* by Paul Gosling. As Co-operative MP and party chair Gareth Thomas puts it, 'local councils don't always spend the time to find out how a co-operative model might work.'[158] Gosling's most prominent case study, of the contracting out of

---

157*   USDAW is the shopworkers trade union.

158   Peter Hunt and Gareth Thomas MP, interviews with the author.

leisure services provision (in Greenwich) to the Greenwich Leisure co-operative has now been replicated in around one hundred other councils, including Salford and Bristol.

The first *New Mutualism* pamphlet, written by journalist Peter Kellner and published in September 1998, boasted a foreword from Tony Blair. For Blair, Kellner's pamphlet was undoubtedly one of many contributions to the debate around the 'Third Way'. Indeed in his preface, Kellner states that he 'first advanced the case for "mutualism" at the Prime Minister's seminar on the Third Way... in May 1998.' But while the Third Way remained a vague, inchoate concept, as much about Blair's media positioning between 'old left and new right', Kellner's essay was firmly rooted in the values of the Co-operative Party as a consumer voice and its critique of state-ism – of Douglas Jay's infamous insistence that 'the gentleman in Whitehall really does know better what is good for people than they do themselves.' Kellner argued:

> *'Socialism as we have come to understand it is not how it started out. The word "socialist" first appeared in November 1827 in the Co-operative magazine – a vehicle for the ideas of Robert Owen who sought to run his textile mill in Lanark on co-operative lines. In Owen's world a socialist was someone who co-operated with others for the common good. He was arguably an unrealistic romantic in his attempt to banish selfish and competitive instincts, but one thing he was not was an advocate of state control... The villain of the piece is Karl Marx. He converted an ethic, to do with fairness, justice and co-operation, into an anti-capitalist ideology that sought public ownership and state control. He was also responsible for implanting the notion of society as a machine... the Marxist legacy has survived, not so much as an economic doctrine but as an outdated way of regarding power, society and the state.'*

For Kellner, Tony Blair had an opportunity to modernise socialism by returning to its real roots, by separating, as Crosland had sought to do, ends and means: 'Government has a duty to promote responsible market behaviour; to act as an effective umpire it should, so far as possible, avoid being a market competitor... government... should, as far as possible leave delivery to independent institutions.'

But the Third Way remained so nebulous as to be meaningless and Blair himself showed little inclination to engage with the detail of modernising socialism. His early endorsement of the 'stakeholder society' espoused by Will Hutton had led commentators to seek to use Hutton's book as a yardstick to judge the success or otherwise of Blair's government. It was not a situation with which Blair was comfortable. Instead, as Downing Street rang to the mantras of 'delivery, delivery, delivery' and 'what matters is what works,' Blair turned to

Lord Birt and secondees from McKinsey: clever technocrats, to whom Douglas Jay's aphorism might well apply as much as it did to the brilliant civil servants of the 1940s. Indeed, they resembled Jay more than they realised for he too had been a temporary civil servant, brought in during the Second World War (just as were Harold Wilson, Hugh Gaitskell and Charles Clarke's father Otto) when for a brief few years the monastic conventions shielding the civil service mandarinate from infiltration by temporary outsiders was lifted.[159] The most 'New Labour' of Co-operative Party ministers were constantly frustrated by the blank incomprehension of otherwise bright civil servants (and management consultants) at the suggestion of co-operative solutions to public policy issues. To them, private versus public was a simpler dichotomy.

Hunt recognised this and took practical action to overcome it. In the past the Co-operative Party had urged Labour-led governments to encourage co-operatives, and relied on the civil servants who advised ministers to work out how this was to be done. Hunt saw that the Co-operative Party would have a greater impact if it could provide the answers to the 'how' question itself. It is this that led to the creation of Mutuo: a Co-operative Party think-tank.

It was more besides. Mutuo also made a virtue of necessity. On becoming General Secretary, Hunt was faced with the news from Graham Melmoth that as part of an economy drive, CWS was seeking to cut its grant to the party. Melmoth told him that he needed to cut a quarter of the £1.2m Co-operative Party budget. Of that £250,000, Hunt persuaded Melmoth into giving £150,000 back in order to set up Mutuo. Hunt's vision was that it would operate in such a way as to bring in consultancy income from operating as a think-tank on wider mutual issues to organisations such as building societies and mutual insurers. Launched in 2000, within seven years it would be turning over £250,000 and no longer needing grant aid.

Adrian Bailey was one of those who believed the lack of sufficient research capability under Peter Clarke to have been a false economy: 'It was increasingly obvious to me and others that the Co-operative Party needed to have more of a think-tank status. We also needed to bring in people from the retail movement and finance sector who couldn't be associated with the Labour Party. Mutuo was born out of that. Peter Hunt deserves a lot of credit for that and the improvement it has made to the quality of literature.'[160] Chancellor Gordon Brown, the former

---

159   The two periods when the British state has operated most effectively were during the two world wars when standard civil service recruitment processes (whereby senior officials start as graduates and work their way up) were overridden and outsiders were brought in directly.

160   Adrian Bailey MP. Interview with the author.

editor of the *New Statesman* Ian Hargreaves and the former Conservative MP and deputy speaker Lord Naseby agreed to be patrons. For Hunt, 'everything Mutuo does needs to have a hard concrete proposal that will either create a new mutual or expand an existing one'.[161] A stream of practical policy proposals emerged over the next few years, including several which have already born fruit.

The first came not strictly from a Mutuo pamphlet but from one of Hunt's original 'freethinking' *New Mutualism* series. This was *New Mutualism – a Golden Goal?* Written by the Sainsbury Professor of Management at Birkbeck, Jonathan Michie, it sought to address the problems arising from the flotation of football clubs. Michie argued that 'what is needed is the mutualisation of football clubs so that they are owned and run by their supporters.' Encouraged by two keen footballers – his PPS, Co-operative MP Andy Reed,[162] and his special adviser Andy Burnham[163] – the Secretary of State for Culture, Media and Sport Chris Smith committed the government to funding an organisation to help this process. In 1999 Supporters Direct was born and a 2003 Mutuo publication *Back Home – Returning Football Clubs to their Communities*, contained a raft of successful case studies. Some 125,000 people have now joined around 140 supporters trusts and supporter-owned clubs including Brentford where the chair is famously Greg Dyke. A more recent Mutuo pamphlet (*The People's Games* – March 2007) also involves sport, proposing a mutual solution to the lack of real accountability surrounding the 2012 Olympics.

Another previously unexplored area for the Co-operative Party in which Mutuo has nevertheless made an impact has been health. *Making Healthcare Mutual*, co-written by Hazel Blears (an enthusiastic and committed Co-operative Party member despite not officially being a Co-operative MP), Peter Hunt and Cliff Mills, was published in 2002. It sought to show how co-operation could provide the key to rejuvenating the creaking management structures of the NHS and sought to harness the opportunity provided by Foundation Trust hospitals for mutualism. It underpinned the only successful non-government amendment to the Foundation Trust hospitals legislation. Proposed by Co-operative MP Adrian Bailey this inserted a requirement on Foundation Trusts to ensure that their membership was actually representative. The narrowness of the government's majority meant that the support of Co-operative MPs was pivotal in securing the passage of the Foundation Trusts legislation.

---

161   Peter Hunt. Interview with the author.

162   Andy Reed, elected MP for Loughborough in 1997 at the age of only thirty-three, has been one of the more prolific sporting enthusiasts of the Blair/Brown parliaments. He subsequently became PPS to Margaret Beckett and Dawn Primarolo. He is currently chair of the Co-operative Party Parliamentary Group.

163   Now a Co-operative Party member and Labour Cabinet minister

A further health service publication was *Care on Call*, which provided a model for asset-locked out-of-hours GP mutuals. Published in January 2004, and launched at the Department of Health by minister John Hutton, it has been taken up by twenty-two out-of-hours mutuals covering approximately a fifth of out-of-hours cover. Also published in 2004 was *Community Engagement in Energy through Mutuals*, by Dr. Gill Owen, an energy policy expert at Warwick University Business School. It argued that co-operative wind-farms could unblock the widespread NIMBY opposition to renewable energy by giving local people a stake in the success of the projects. The first co-operative wind farm – in Oxfordshire – is now up and running, and Alun Michael, who contributed a foreword to the pamphlet in his role as minister of state at DEFRA, organised a parliamentary debate during the summer of 2006 to highlight the issue.

Child's Play, a Mutuo publication produced with support from DFES, provided a model for a mutual Surestart scheme based upon the Millmead Surestart in Folkestone founded by Cliff Mills. Further Mutuo work for young people has included another proposal now implemented. This is *Co-operation in Learning* which suggested a network of a dozen specialist business and enterprise schools sponsored by the Co-operative Group supported by curriculum materials to enable GCSE and Key Stage projects on co-operatives and mutuals. The network has now been successfully operating for three years.

An important area of Mutuo work during 2007 has been on employee ownership. Sarah McCarthy-Fry, a new Co-operative MP and the chair of a working-group on the issue believes: 'The driving principles that make co-operatives work are employee involvement in the future and the direction of the company. Even though they are not necessarily technically a co-operative the issue relates to co-operative principles. It's our Clause IV moment – the same step. It's no longer about making everything technically a cooperative. It's about thinking outside the box about how we can use co-operative principles – such as in foundation hospitals. It's about democratising the big state-run organisations. The Post Office, for example – that would work better run as a co-operative.'[164]

Another Mutuo project has addressed one of the traditional totemic issues of the Co-operative Party, developing a new business model for better-run co-operative housing. In the past, problems have arisen in some co-operatives with the hijacking of committees by unrepresentative but vocal minorities, who have created division and discontent by imposing their views on the rest of the membership. This made many building societies and banks reluctant to lend money to co-operative housing ventures. Mutuo developed a new model, the Community Housing Mutual, also known as the Community Housing Gateway, under which housing stock is transferred to a body owned by the tenants, but not managed directly by them. Building societies who were reluctant to lend to

---

164   Sarah McCarthy-Fry, interview with the author.

housing co-operatives run on traditional lines have welcomed this approach. It is now the preferred model of the Welsh Assembly government and is being explored in places ranging from Swansea and Rhonda Cynon Taff via Preston to Watford and Hertsmere.

Mutuo has given added credibility to Co-operative Party policy papers. It has enabled Co-operative Party MPs to operate more effectively than ever before in making use of the opportunities afforded by a friendly government to secure legislative changes through private members bills. The 2001 general election returned four additional Co-operative Party MPs. Allowing for the retirement of the veteran MP Alf Morris and the untimely death of Gordon McMaster, this took the Co-operative parliamentary group to a record size of thirty.

Following the election, the names of two Co-operative MPs were drawn amongst the top seven in the annual ballot for private members bills. This guaranteed them sufficient parliamentary time to propose bills with a reasonable chance of their becoming law. One of these MPs was Mark Lazarowicz.[164*] His Bill, which became the Employee Share Schemes Act in 2002, realised the aspirations of the March 2001 Mutuo paper written by Jonathan Michie and fellow academic Christine Oughton on employee share ownership, *Employees Direct*. It helped fulfil the government's generalised enthusiasm for employee share schemes, firstly by creating democratic employee share trusts so that employee-held shares could be democratically managed and secondly by changing the corporate tax relief regime so that employers who transferred shares to employees would no longer have to wait six years to receive tax relief.

The other MP was Gareth Thomas at Harrow West. Only twenty-nine on his election to parliament in 1997, in 2000 he had been elected chair of the Co-operative Party – becoming only the third MP to have held the position.[165] Thomas's bill became the Industrial and Provident Societies Act 2002. Firstly it improved protection for co-operative societies against de-mutualisation by increasing the threshold of members whose support was required for such a decision to be taken. Secondly it altered the Industrial and Provident Societies Act 1968 to allow it to be amended in future by Statutory Instrument. This was a groundbreaking achievement in that it meant that no longer would primary legislation and months of parliamentary time be required to update or amend the legislation governing mutuals and co-operatives. It had been this very rock

---

164*   Born in Dagenham, Lazarowicz had become involved in both Labour and Co-operative politics in Scotland where he had been chair of St Andrews University Labour Club, leader of Edinburgh City Council 1986-93 and chair of the Scottish Labour Party 1989-90.

165   A former schoolteacher, Thomas had been elected to Harrow council in his early twenties.

– the inability to secure sufficient parliamentary time for the scale of primary legislation envisaged – on which Peter Clarke's proposed Co-operatives Bill, had foundered in 1997. Clarke had been unable to surmount the obstacle. Thomas had found a way around it.

Two more Mutuo inspired private members bills followed. The first was put through parliament by Mark Todd MP during 2002 and became the Co-operatives and Community Benefit Societies Act 2003. Though Todd was a Labour as opposed to a Co-operative Party MP, he was an enthusiastic party member and had been a director of the old Cambridge Co-operative Society.[166] The Todd bill introduced an asset-lock on community benefit organisations which, along with co-operatives, were the main organisations covered by industrial and provident society legislation.[167] Indeed, there was an achievement for the co-operative movement in the Todd bill's name. The phrase 'industrial and provident' symbolised for many co-operators the reluctance of civil servants to recognise the significance of the co-operative movement. It implied that co-operatives were but a small species of fish in the vast pool of industrial and provident organisations. In reality, there was little else that industrial and provident legislation covered apart from co-operatives or community benefit organisations. As one senior Co-operative Party figure put it: 'What the co-operative movement wanted was recognition. That was one reason why the 1990s Co-operatives Bill came to be seen as totemic by many activists.'[168]

The most recent of the four private members bills, the Building Societies (Funding) and Mutual Societies (Transfers) Bill was introduced to the Commons in December 2006 by Conservative MP John Butterfill and has been making progress through parliament during 2007. Butterfill is vice-chair of the All Party Parliamentary Building Societies and Financial Mutuals Group, of which Mutuo

166   Cambridge was one of the regional co-operative societies now merged into the CRS and thence into the Co-operative Group. Todd had also been leader of Cambridge City Council. He had been MP for South Derbyshire since defeating Edwina Currie in 1997.

167   Greenwich Leisure (founded 1992) and football supporters trusts are community benefit organisations (bencomms), not technically co-operatives, because they are not a member benefit organisation. Co-op members own capital value, bencomm members don't. Co-ops are not social enterprises, as they can be sold by their members. Community Benefit Societies are social enterprises – like Greenwich Leisure. To put public assets in them requires an asset-lock to ensure that they cannot be converted into a private company. Officials had tried to reinvent the wheel with concept of a Community Interest Company (CIC) – co-ops were seen as fusty by civil servants. But the CIC is essentially the same as a co-op or community benefit society, except that it has asset-lock. The CIC asset lock is the same as that introduced by the Todd bill, but the CIC is governed by company law.

168   Interview with the author.

provides the secretariat. The first part of the Bill helps building societies compete on a level playing field with banks as mortgage lenders.[169] The second part gives members and wholesale funders equal rights should a building society go bust. Under current legislation, wholesale lenders (i.e. the banks) are first in the queue. The third part provides further mitigation against the pressure to demutualise by making it easier for mutuals of different types to amalgamate and rationalise.[170]

For Sarah McCarthy-Fry, one of the new Co-operative MPs elected at the 2005 election, 'the big achievement of the Co-operative Parliamentary Group since 1997 has been to get a level playing field for mutual businesses. People have this blanket idea that a nationalised industry would protect workers. But real socialism is about co-operation. It's about people, not structure. The Co-operative Parliamentary Group is now punching above its weight.'[171] That impact has perhaps been most strikingly manifest in the *Review of the GB co-operative and credit union legislation* announced by the then Economic Secretary to the Treasury, Ed Balls, who with Sarah McCarthy-Fry at Portsmouth North, Linda Riorden at Halifax and Meg Hillier at Hackney South was one of four new Co-operative Party MPs elected at the 2005 election. Balls's review harnessed the so-called 'Thomas power,'[172] under which government can now amend legislation governing co-operatives by means of Statutory Instruments which by convention do not need the parliamentary time required to pass primary legislation. The consultation process begun by Balls therefore provides a realistic opportunity to realise the aspirations of the stillborn draft Co-operative Bill of the early 1990s. In 1997, recalls the Co-operative Parliamentary Group chair Andy Reed, 'people were perhaps over-optimistic – there was the belief

---

169   It was originally suggested by the All-Party Group inquiry into the costs of demutualisation. Building societies must have a minimum of 50% of assets held by members. This means that they are limited in what they can lend in mortgages in a way banks are not as Building societies are unable to borrow more than a certain limit. The bill give powers to the Treasury to vary this limit above 50% (but no higher than 75%). This would enable them to compete on a level playing field with banks, who are not similarly constrained, in delivering the cheapest possible mortgages. By creating a more level playing field between building societies and banks it mitigates a commercial pressure to de-mutualise.

170   Currently a building society can merge more favourably with another building society than with a friendly soc, or a co-op for example. The bill levels the playing field, so that instead of treating a merger between a building society and say a co-operative as a demutualisation it is recognised as being not. It tackles demarcation lines and silo legislation between different types of mutuals.

171   Sarah McCarthy-Fry, interview with the author.

172   Named after Gareth Thomas's private members bill which introduced it.

that the co-operative agenda could be rolled out in one easy sweep.' Ted
Graham agrees: 'Gareth Thomas, Peter Hunt and Ed Balls have done piecemeal
what the idea of the Co-operative Bill was trying to do for the previous
decade.'[173]

With Gordon Brown Prime Minister, the Co-operative Party arguably finds
itself in at its strongest political position yet.[174] Its parliamentary strength stands
at twenty-nine, one down on the record thirty of 2001. Its representation in
government is stronger than ever before. In the past it has tended either to lack
a Cabinet-level minister or else (as in the AV Alexander era), it has had few
credible alternative stars to the single 'Mr Co-op'.[175] Gordon Brown has been
able to promote a team of younger Co-operative MPs at junior ministerial level[176]
to augment the influence enjoyed by Ed Balls – only the third Cabinet minister
in Co-operative Party history. At the same time Gareth Thomas, the chair of the
Co-operative Party since 2000, as George Foulkes observes, has 'broken barriers
– he was chair of Congress early and has not let being a minister restrain his co-
operative instincts'.[177] Additionally the Co-operative Party has four MPs in some
of the most influential non-ministerial positions: Tommy McAvoy is now the
longest serving government pairing whip in history; Barry Sheerman and John
McFall are respectively chairs of the education and treasury select committees
and Angela Smith is PPS to the Prime Minister (the second Co-operative MP to
fulfil the role of PPS to Gordon Brown since 1997).

The Co-operative Party's influence under Gordon Brown's premiership is also
in the realm of ideas. Brown is an instinctive co-operator, and the first Party
member to become Prime Minister. For George Foulkes, now an active Co-
operative Peer and an MSP having served as a minister 1997-2002, 'the last ten
years has seen a renaissance in the co-operative ideal'.[178] As Chancellor, Brown
could support and encourage this. It was under Brown's chancellorship after all,
that Balls launched the review of co-operative and credit union legislation (and
a £30m fund to support credit unions in squeezing out loan sharks). Brown's
premiership is a unique and unprecedented opportunity for the Co-operative
Party.

Geoff Mulgan observed in the July 2007 issue of *Prospect* that:

---

173   Andy Reed and Lord Graham, interviews with the author.
174   This is despite a tight funding situation having forced the closure of its offices in the
       English regions.
175   In the past this has invariably been a Mr rather than a Ms Co-op.
176   Gareth Thomas as under-secretary for trade and consumer affairs, Meg Hillier as under-
       secretary at the Home Office, Meg Munn as under-secretary at the Foreign Office, and
       Phil Hope as Minister for the Third Sector – a crucial appointment for a Co-operative MP
       in that the brief includes responsibility for policy on co-operatives and mutuals.
177   Lord Foulkes, interview with the author.
178   Lord Foulkes, interview with the author.

'For [Brown], politics is about helping society to act as a moral community rather than just as a collection of individuals. This was not a viewpoint shared by most of the centre-left British political intelligentsia during the 1980s and 1990s, for whom morality was a matter of personal taste, and much less important than constitutional reform or novel economic strategies. Brown, by contrast, felt that without an account of what it is in human nature that makes people co-operative, and what it is in human institutions that reinforces those dispositions, the left would always be on the defensive.'

Brown's international agenda is rooted in the same ethical framework which led the Co-operative Party to be an early advocate of a trade boycott of apartheid South-Africa and of the fair trade agenda pioneered by co-operative retail.

On the domestic front the opportunity is there for co-operative ideas to inform more effective solutions than Blair managed to the challenges facing the government. As Andy Reed puts it, 'the government needs to think outside the box on the way we deliver.' For Sarah McCarthy-Fry, 'the themes that Gordon is bringing forward reflect co-operative ideas such as devolution to communities and giving people the tools to participate effectively.' In the Blair cabinet, there were several Labour ministers keen to harness co-operative ideas. Hazel Blears, who organised seminars[179] for ministers to learn about Co-operative Party ideas was prime among them. Four out of the six contenders in the 2007 Labour deputy leadership election are actually members of the Co-operative Party (Hazel, Hilary, Hain and Harman). Including Brown and Balls, ten of the Cabinet are now Co-operative Party members, the others being David.Miliband, the four deputy leadership candidates just mentioned, and three of the new young MPs promoted to cabinet for the first time by Brown: Andy Burnham, Ed Miliband and James Purnell. Brown has become prime minister at a historic moment for Labour. Andy Love argues: 'In my view, the role of the Co-operative Party is ensuring that the bias towards a producer-oriented politics would be mitigated by a consumerist view. The Labour government has shifted from getting into bed with the trade unions and together improving public services, to looking at it from a consumer point of view. The wellspring for that thinking came from co-operative ideas. The Co-operative Party helped make them respectable.'[180] It is a historic opportunity for a Co-operative Party ninety years young.

---

179   For example on securing greater citizen involvement in public services.
180   Andy Reed, Sarah McCarhy-Fry and Andy Love, interviews with the author.

ACKNOWLEDGMENTS

Unless otherwise stated quotations are from conference reports or from interviews conducted by the author either in person or over the telephone during the period May-July 2007. I am grateful to the following who at short notice were kind enough to give of their time, recollections and insights:

Adrian Bailey MP; Tom Carbery; Jim Craigen; Louise Ellman MP; Rt. Hon Lord Foulkes; Rt. Hon Lord Graham of Edmonton; Peter Hunt; Rt. Hon Baroness Jay; Andy Love MP; Rt. Hon Dickson Mabon; Sarah McCarthy-Fry MP; Rt. Hon. Alun Michael MP; Stan Newens; Lady Joan Oram; Andy Reed MP; Rita Rhodes; Marion Rilstone; Barry Sheerman MP; Angela Smith MP; Rt. Hon. John Spellar MP; Gareth Thomas MP; Lord Thomas of Macclesfield; Richard Tomlinson; and David Wise.

For their assistance with my research and the production of the book, I am grateful to Roger Bennett, Chris Booth, Hilda Carr, Jim Craigen, Robbie Erbmann, George Foulkes, Ted Graham, Peter Hunt, Lord Macintosh of Haringey, Professor the Lord Morgan; Helen Pyper, Rita Rhodes, Marion Rilstone, John Schwartz, Ron Atkin; and staff of Bishopsgate Library, the Co-operative archive in Manchester, the People's History Museum and the British Library. For their forbearance over the past few months I would also like to thank Mark, Tamsin, Daniel, Sophie, Phil and Charlotte.

For their insights I am grateful to Tom Carbery, Stan Newens and Rita Rhodes, whose histories of the Co-operative Party, the LCS and the RACS were invaluable; and to Jon Henderson of the *Observer* for his generosity in sharing the draft first chapter of his forthcoming biography of Fred Perry.

For their encouragement and enthusiasm for this book, I am particularly indebted to Gareth Thomas MP, and to Peter Hunt and Ted Graham whose kindness in looking over early drafts saved the author from several errors of fact, and to Georgina Pattinson, who adjusted to living with the Co-operative Party impressively swiftly and whose patience and heroic enthusiasm in assisting with the proofing process went above and beyond the call of duty.

BIBLIOGRAPHY AND FURTHER READING

The only full history of the Co-operative Party was written during the late 1960s by Tom Carbery, a professor at Strathclyde University. Entitled *Consumers in Politics – A history and general review of the Co-operative Party*, it is informative, well written and detailed. It was published by Manchester University Press in 1969.

Geoffrey Rhodes, who was a Co-operative Party MP from 1964 until his early death in 1974 published a shorter work entitled *Co-operative Labour Relations 1900-1962* (Co-operative College Paper 8, Co-operative Union).

GDH Cole, *A Century of Co-operation* (Co-operative Union, 1944) includes a chapter on co-operative politics.

Rita Rhodes, formerly Lecturer in Co-operative Studies at the University of Ulster published a history of the Royal Arsenal Co-operative Society entitled *An Arsenal for Labour – The Royal Arsenal Co-operative Society and Politics 1896-1996* (Co-operative Union, 1998).

Stan Newens, an ex-MP and former president of the London Co-operative Society published *Working Together – A short History of the London Co-operative Society Political Committee.* (CRS London Political Committee, 1988)

Memoirs and biographies of significant Co-operative Party politicians include:
Churchill's Favourite Socialist – a biography of AV Alexander by former Co-operative MP John Tilley;
From Tyne to Thames – Via the Usual Channels, by Lord Graham of Edmonton (The Memoir Club, 2005);
An Autobiography by Fred Perry (Hutchinson, 1984) which contains useful chapters on his father and early campaigning;
Death of an Idealist, a memoir by John Stonehouse (London, 1975).

There are also biographies of several Co-operative Party politicians including AV Alexander, Ed Balls, Ted Graham, Dickson Mabon, Alun Michael and John Stonehouse in the *Dictionary of Labour Biography* (ed. Greg Rosen) published by Politicos in 2001.

Other books dealing with the history and personalities of the Co-operative Party include: Bernard Donoughue and George Jones, *Herbert Morrison – Portrait of a Politician*, (London 1973); Greg Rosen, *Old Labour to New*, (Politicos Publishing, 2005).

CO-OPERATIVE MPS SINCE THE BIRTH OF THE CO-OPERATIVE PARTY

1918	A. E. Waterson	Kettering
1922	A. V. Alexander	Sheffield Hillsborough
	A. Barnes	East Ham South
	T. Henderson	Glasgow Tradeston
	R. C. Morrison	Tottenham North
1923	A. V. Alexander	Sheffield Hillsborough
	A. Barnes	East Ham South
	T. Henderson	Glasgow Tradeston
	R. C. Morrison	Tottenham North
	S. F. Perry	Kettering
	A. Young	Glasgow Partick
1924	A. V. Alexander	Sheffield Hillsborough
	A. Barnes	East Ham South
	T. Henderson	Glasgow Tradeston
	W. Hirst	Bradford South
	R. C. Morrison	Tottenham North
1929	A. V. Alexander	Sheffield Hillsborough
	A. Barnes	East Ham South
	D. Chater	Hammersmith South
	H. M. Gibson	Mossley
	T. Henderson	Glasgow Tradeston
	W. Hirst	Bradford South
	F. Longden	Birmingham
	R. C. Morrison	Tottenham North
	S. F. Perry	Kettering
1931	W. Leonard	Glasgow St Rollox
1935	A. V. Alexander	Sheffield Hillsborough
	A. Barnes	East Ham South
	D. Chater	Bethnal Green North East
	F. A. Broad	Edmonton
	W. H. Green	Deptford
	T. Henderson	Glasgow Tradeston
	W. Leonard	Glasgow St Rollox
	R. C. Morrison	Tottenham North
	Rev. G. S. Woods	Finsbury
1945	W. T. Adams	Hammersmith South
	A. V. Alexander	Sheffield Hillsborough
	A. Barnes	East Ham South
	Flt/Lt F. Beswick	Uxbridge
	D. Chater	Bethnal Green North East

W. Coldrick	Bristol North
P. Daines	East Ham North
N. Dodds	Dartford
J. C. Forman	Glasgow Springburn
Mrs C. S. Ganley	Battersea South
P. Holman	Bethnal Green South West
J. H. Hudson	Ealing West
W. Leonard	Glasgow St Rollox
F. Longden	Birmingham Deritend
R. C. Morrison	Tottenham North
W. Nally	Wolverhampton Bilston
J. Rankin	Glasgow Tradeston
Mrs M. Ridealgh	Ilford North
H. Norman Smith	Nottingham South
S. Tiffany	Peterborough
M. F. Titterington	Bradford South
Mrs E. A. Wills	Birmingham Duddeston
Rev. G. S. Woods	Mossley

1950

A. Barnes	East Ham South
F. Beswick	Uxbridge
W. Coldrick	Bristol North East
P. Daines	East Ham, North
G. Darling	Sheffield Hillsborough
N. Dodds	Dartford
J. C. Forman	Glasgow Springburn
Mrs C. S. Ganley	Battersea South
P. Holman	Bethnal Green
J. Hudson	Ealing North
W. Irving	Wood Green
F. Longden	Birmingham Small Heath
F. Messer	Tottenham
W. Nally	Bilston
J. Rankin	Glasgow Tradeston
H. N. Smith	Nottingham South
W. T. Williams	Hammersmith South
Rev. G. S. Woods	Droylsden

1951

A. Barnes	East Ham North
F. Beswick	Uxbridge
W. Coldrick	Bristol North East
P. Daines	East Ham South
G. Darling	Sheffield Hillsborough
N. Dodds	Dartford
J. Forman	Glasgow Springburn
P. Holman	Bethnal Green
J. Hudson	Ealing North
W. Irving	Wood Green
F. Longden	Birmingham Small Heath
F. Messer	Tottenham
W. Nally	Bilston
J. Rankin	Glasgow Tradeston
H. N. Smith	Nottingham South
W. T. Williams	Hammersmith South

1955	F. Beswick	Uxbridge
	Mrs J. Butler	Wood Green
	W. Coldrick	Bristol North East
	P. Daines	East Ham North
	G. Darling	Sheffield Hillsborough
	N. Dodds	Erith & Crayford
	R. Edwards	Bilston
	J. C. Forman	Glasgow Springburn
	P. Holman	Bethnal Green
	S. Irving	Dartford
	R. Ledger	Romford
	Sir Fred Messer	Tottenham
	A. E. Oram	East Ham South
	W. Owen	Morpeth
	A. M. F. Palmer	Cleveland
	J. Rankin	Glasgow Govan
	Mrs Harriet Slater	Stoke-on-Trent North
	W. E. Wheeldon	Birmingham Small Heath
	W. T. Williams	Barons Court
1959	Mrs J. Butler	Wood Green
	G. Darling	Sheffield Hillsborough
	N. Dodds	Erith & Crayford
	R. Edwards	Bilston
	J. Forman	Glasgow Springburn
	P. Holman	Bethnal Green
	S. Irving	Dartford
	R. Ledger	Romford
	Dr J. Dickson Mabon	Greenock
	A. E. Oram	East Ham South
	W. Owen	Morpeth
	L. Pavitt	Willesden West
	J. Rankin	Glasgow Govan
	Mrs Harriet Slater	Stoke-on-Trent North
	J. Stonehouse	Wednesbury
	W. Wheeldon	Birmingham Small Heath
1964	Mrs J. Butler	Wood Green
	G. Darling	Sheffield Hillsborough
	N. Dodds	Erith & Crayford
	R. Edwards	Bilston
	I. Evans	Birmingham Yardley
	P. Holman	Bethnal Green
	S. Irving	Dartford
	R. Ledger	Romford
	Dr. J. Dickson Mabon	Greenock
	A. Morris	Manchester Wythenshawe
	A. E. Oram	East Ham South
	W. Owen	Morpeth
	A. Palmer	Bristol Central
	L. Pavitt	Willesden West
	J. Rankin	Glasgow Govan
	G. Rhodes	Newcastle East
	Mrs Harriet Slater	Stoke-on-Trent North

J. Stonehouse	Wednesbury
W. T. Williams	Warrington

1966

Mrs J. Butler	Wood Green
G. Darling	Sheffield Hillsborough
R. Edwards	Bilston
I. Evans	Birmingham Yardley
C. N. Haseldine	Bradford West
W. Hilton	Bethnal Green
S. Irving	Dartford
R. Ledger	Romford
Dr J. Dickson Mabon	Greenock
A. Morris	Manchester Whythenshawe
A. E. Oram	East Ham South
W. Owen	Morpeth
A. Palmer	Bristol Central
L. Pavitt	Willesden West
J. Rankin	Glasgow Govan
G. Rhodes	Newcastle East
J. Stonehouse	Wednesbury
W. T. Williams	Warrington

1970

Joyce Butler	Wood Green
George Darling	Sheffield Hillsborough
Dick Douglas	Stirlingshire East and Clackmannan
Bob Edwards	Bilston
Bill Hilton	Bethnal Green
Dickson Mabon	Greenock
Alf Morris	Manchester Wythenshawe
Bert Oram	East Ham South
Arthur Palmer	Bristol Central
Laurie Pavitt	Willesden West
John Rankin	Glasgow Govan
Geoffrey Rhodes	Newcastle East
John Roper	Farnworth
John Stonehouse	Wednesbury
Tom Williams	Warrington

1974 (Feb)

Ioan Evans	Aberdare
Laurie Pavitt	Brent South
Arthur M. F. Palmer	Bristol North East
Sydney Irving	Dartford
Ted Graham	Enfield Edmonton
John Roper	Farnworth
James M. Craigen	Glasgow Maryhill
Dr J. Dickson Mabon	Greenock and Port Glasgow
Stan Newens	Harlow
Alfred Morris	Manchester Wythenshawe
Michael Thomas	Newcastle on Tyne East
Ian Wrigglesworth	Teeside Thornaby
W. T. Williams	Warrington
Bob Edwards	Wolverhampton South East

1974 (Oct)	Ioan Evans	Aberdare
	Laurie Pavitt	Brent South
	Arthur M. F. Palmer	Bristol North East
	Sydney Irving	Dartford
	Ted Graham	Enfield Edmonton
	John Roper	Farnworth
	James M. Craigen	Glasgow Maryhill
	Dr J. Dickson Mabon	Greenock and Port Glasgow
	Stan Newens	Harlow
	Alfred Morris	Manchester Wythenshawe
	Michael Thomas	Newcastle on Tyne East
	Ian Wrigglesworth	Teeside Thornaby
	W. T. Williams	Warrington
	Bob Edwards	Wolverhampton South East
1979	Ioan Evans	Aberdare
	Laurie Pavitt	Brent South
	Arthur M. F. Palmer	Bristol North East
	Ted Graham	Enfield Edmonton
	John Roper	Farnworth
	James M. Craigen	Glasgow Maryhill
	Dr J. Dickson Mabon	Greenock and Port Glasgow
	Stan Newens	Harlow
	Alfred Morris	Manchester Wythenshawe
	Michael Thomas	Newcastle on Tyne East
	Ian Wrigglesworth	Teeside Thornaby
	Bob Edwards	Wolverhampton South East
	Richard G. Douglas	Dunfermline
	Barry J. Sheerman	Huddersfield East
	John Tilley	Lambeth Central
	George Foulkes	South Ayrshire
	Sir Thomas Williams	Warrington
1983 (Mar-Jun)	Ossie O'Brien	Darlington
1983	Jim Craigen	Glasgow, Maryhill
	Dick Douglas	Dunfermline West
	Robert Edwards	Wolverhampton South East
	Ioan Evans	Cynon Valley
	George Foulkes	Carrick, Cumnock & Doon Valley
	Laurie Pavitt	Brent South
	Barry Sheerman	Huddersfield
1987	Dick Douglas	Dunfermline West
	George Foulkes	Carrick, Cumnock & Doon Valley
	Thomas McAvoy	Glasgow, Rutherglen
	John McFall	Dumbarton
	Alun Michael	Cardiff South & Penarth
	Alf Morris	Manchester Whythenshawe
	Lewis Moonie	Kirkcaldy
	Barry Sheerman	Huddersfield
	Dennis Turner	Wolverhampton South East

1992	Ian Davidson	Glasgow Govan
	George Foulkes	Carrick, Cumnock & Doon Valley
	Mike Gapes	Ilford South
	Jon Owen Jones	Cardiff Central
	Alan Keen	Feltham & Heston
	Tom McAvoy	Glasgow, Rutherglen
	John McFall	Dumbarton
	Gordon McMaster	Paisley South
	Alun Michael	Cardiff South & Penarth
	Lewis Moonie	Kirkcaldy
	Alfred Morris	Manchester Wythenshawe
	Ken Purchase	Wolverhampton North East
	Barry Sheerman	Huddersfield
	Dennis Turner	Wolverhampton South East
1997	Ian Davidson	Glasgow, Pollok
	Jim Dobbin	Heywood & Middleton
	David Drew	Stroud
	Louise Ellman	Liverpool, Riverside
	George Foulkes	Carrick, Cumnock & Doon Valley
	Mike Gapes	Ilford South
	Linda Gilroy	Plymouth, Sutton
	Phil Hope	Corby
	Jon Owen Jones	Cardiff Central
	Alan Keen	Feltham & Heston
	David Lepper	Brighton, Pavilion
	Andy Love	Edmonton
	Thomas McAvoy	Glasgow, Rutherglen
	John McFall	Dumbarton
	Gordon McMaster	Paisley South
	Tony McWalter	Hemel Hempstead
	Alun Michael	Cardiff South & Penarth
	Lewis Moonie	Kirkcaldy
	Alfred Morris	Manchester Wythenshawe
	Doug Naysmith	Bristol North West
	Ken Purchase	Wolverhampton North East
	Andy Reed	Loughborough
	Barry Sheerman	Huddersfield
	Angela E. Smith	Basildon
	David Taylor	North West Leicestershire
	Gareth Thomas	Harrow West
	Don Touhig	Islwyn
	Dennis Turner	Wolverhampton South East
2001	Adrian Bailey	West Bromwich West
	Ian Davidson	Glasgow, Govan
	Jim Dobbin	Heywood and Middleton
	David Drew	Stroud
	Louise Ellman	Liverpool Riverside
	George Foulkes	Carrick, Cumnock and Doon Valley
	Mike Gapes	Ilford South
	Linda Gilroy	Plymouth South
	Mark Hendrick	Preston
	Phil Hope	Corby

Jon Owen Jones	Cardiff Central
Alan Keen	Feltham and Heston
Mark Lazarowicz	Edinburgh North and Leith
David Lepper	Brighton Pavilion
Andy Love	Edmonton
Thomas McAvoy	Glasgow, Rutherglen
John McFall	Dumbarton
Tony McWalter	Hemel Hempstead
Alun Michael	Cardiff South and Penarth
Lewis Moonie	Kirkaldy
Meg Munn	Sheffield Heeley
Doug Naysmith	Bristol North West
Ken Purchase	Wolverhampton North East
Andy Reed	Loughborough
Barry Sheerman	Huddersfield
Angela Smith	Basildon
David Taylor	Leicestershire North West
Gareth Thomas	Harrow West
Don Touhig	Islwyn
Dennis Turner	Wolverhampton South East

2005	Adrian Bailey	West Bromwich West
	Ed Balls	Normanton
	Ian Davidson	Glasgow, Govan
	Jim Dobbin	Heywood and Middleton
	David Drew	Stroud
	Louise Ellman	Liverpool Riverside
	Mike Gapes	Ilford South
	Linda Gilroy	Plymouth South
	Mark Hendrick	Preston
	Meg Hillier	Hackney South and Shoreditch
	Phil Hope	Corby
	Alan Keen	Feltham and Heston
	Mark Lazarowicz	Edinburgh North and Leith
	David Lepper	Brighton Pavilion
	Andy Love	Edmonton
	Thomas McAvoy	Glasgow, Rutherglen
	Sarah McCarthy-Fry	Portsmouth North
	John McFall	Dumbarton
	Alun Michael	Cardiff South and Penarth
	Meg Munn	Sheffield Heeley
	Doug Naysmith	Bristol North West
	Ken Purchase	Wolverhampton North East
	Andy Reed	Loughborough
	Linda Riordan	Halifax
	Barry Sheerman	Huddersfield
	Angela Smith	Basildon
	David Taylor	Leicestershire North West
	Gareth Thomas	Harrow West
	Don Touhig	Islwyn

INDEX

References such as "78–9" indicate (not necessarily continuous) discussion across a range of pages, whilst "73n162" indicates a reference to note 162 on page 73 and "73nn" refers to multiple notes on page 73. Wherever possible in the case of topics with many references, these have either been divided into sub-topics (indented below the main heading) or the most significant discussion of the topic is indicated by page numbers in bold. Publication titles are in italics.